W9-AYR-722

GEORGE W. BUSH

Titles in the United States Presidents *series:*

ABRAHAM LINCOLN
ISBN 0-89490-939-8

ANDREW JACKSON
ISBN 0-89490-831-6

ANDREW JOHNSON
ISBN 0-7660-1034-1

BILL CLINTON,
Revised Edition
ISBN 0-7660-2032-0

DWIGHT D. EISENHOWER
ISBN 0-89490-940-1

FRANKLIN D. ROOSEVELT
ISBN 0-7660-1038-4

GEORGE WASHINGTON
ISBN 0-89490-832-4

HARRY S. TRUMAN,
Revised Edition
ISBN 0-7660-2010-X

HERBERT HOOVER
ISBN 0-7660-1035-X

JAMES MADISON
ISBN 0-89490-834-0

JAMES MONROE
ISBN 0-89490-941-X

JAMES K. POLK
ISBN 0-7660-1037-6

JIMMY CARTER
ISBN 0-89490-935-5

JOHN F. KENNEDY
ISBN 0-7660-1039-2

LYNDON B. JOHNSON
ISBN 0-89490-938-X

RICHARD M. NIXON,
Revised Edition
ISBN 0-7660-2031-2

RONALD REAGAN
ISBN 0-89490-835-9

THEODORE ROOSEVELT
ISBN 0-89490-836-7

THOMAS JEFFERSON
ISBN 0-89490-837-5

WOODROW WILSON
ISBN 0-89490-936-3

United States Presidents

GEORGE W. BUSH

Series Consultant:
Don M. Coerver, professor of history
Texas Christian University, Fort Worth, Texas

Sandra J. Kachurek

Enslow Publishers, Inc.

40 Industrial Road	PO Box 38
Box 398	Aldershot
Berkeley Heights, NJ 07922	Hants GU12 6BP
USA	UK

http://www.enslow.com

This book is dedicated to my lovely mother Agnes,
who has always encouraged me to try.

Library of Congress Cataloging-in-Publication Data

    Kachurek, Sandra J.
      George W. Bush / Sandra J. Kachurek.
     p. cm. — (United States presidents)
     Summary: Discusses the life and political career of George W. Bush, up
through the events of September 11, 2001, and the subsequent War on Terror.
     Includes bibliographical references and index.
     ISBN 0-7660-2040-1
     1. Bush, George W. (George Walker), 1946—-Juvenile literature.
    2. Presidents—United States—Biography—Juvenile literature. [1. Bush,
George W. (George Walker), 1946- 2. Presidents.] I. Title. II. Series.
    E903.K33 2004
    973.931'092—dc22

                               2003019539

Printed in the United States of America

10 9 8 7 6 5 4 3 2 1

To Our Readers:
We have done our best to make sure all Internet Addresses in this book were active and
appropriate when we went to press. However, the author and the publisher have no
control over and assume no liability for the material available on those Internet sites
or on other Web sites they may link to. Any comments or suggestions can be sent by
e-mail to comments@enslow.com or to the address on the back cover.

Every effort has been made to locate all copyright holders of material used in this
book. If any errors or omissions have occurred, corrections will be made in future
editions of this book.

Illustration Credits: Courtesy of BushCountry.org, pp. 6, 77, 90, 104, 108;
Corel Corporation, p. 9; George Bush Presidential Library, pp. 16, 19, 26,
32, 38, 40, 42, 43, 46, 52, 53, 100; Library of Congress, p. 62.

Source Documents: Library of Congress, p. 69; www.whitehouse.gov,
pp. 13, 75, 85, 88, 96.

Cover Illustration: Courtesy of BushCountry.org.

CONTENTS

George W. Bush was in office for only eight months when tragedy struck America.

1

"TODAY OUR NATION SAW EVIL"

September 11, 2001 became the day that changed America. It also became the day that defined George W. Bush's early presidency. He had only been in office for eight months.

In Sarasota, Florida, that September Tuesday began hot and humid. The heat did not stop President George W. Bush from running his regular two-mile morning jog.

Hoping to create support for his education bill, President Bush was in Florida visiting Emma E. Booker Elementary School. Sixteen second graders in Sandra Kay Daniels's class were to read for the president.

At 9 A.M. just before Bush entered the classroom, he received a call from his national security adviser in Washington, D.C., Condoleezza Rice. She relayed the news that a plane had crashed into the World Trade Center in New York City. White House officials considered the crash an accident.

Although the news was serious, President Bush looked relaxed and smiled as he sat down to listen to the children read. Less than ten minutes later, however, Andrew Card, White House chief of staff, whispered in the president's ear that a second plane had slammed into a second tower of the World Trade Center. The crashes were no longer considered accidents, but terrorist attacks.

George W. Bush became tense and serious. Although he nodded and continued to listen to the children, he was distracted. At the end, he congratulated the class and quickly left.

In another room at the school, President Bush and his staff watched the television coverage of the World Trade Center attacks and spoke by phone with the White House staff. They told him that the plane crashed at 8:46 A.M. American Flight 11, originally headed from Boston to Los Angeles, had been hijacked and crashed into the high north tower of the World Trade Center. The staff also said that sixteen minutes later, another plane crashed at 9:02 A.M. United Flight 175, also bound to Los Angeles from Boston, had been hijacked and crashed into the south tower of the World Trade Center. All the lives of those on the planes were lost. Rescue workers and firefighters were at the scene or rushing to it.[1]

At 9:30 A.M., President George W. Bush spoke before television cameras in the Booker School's media center. He said, "Terrorism against our nation will not stand."[2]

The President was then sped away to Sarasota Bradenton International Airport where his presidential jet, *Air Force One*, waited for him.

Another shock hit the country and the president, when at 9:38 A.M., American Airlines Flight 77, scheduled to fly from Dulles Airport in Virginia, just outside of Washington, D.C., to Los Angeles, slammed into the southwest side of the Pentagon. The Pentagon is in Virginia. Many of the country's top military officers and government personnel, including Secretary of

The World Trade Center towers (center of photo) were destroyed in a terrorist attack September 11, 2001.

Defense Donald H. Rumsfeld, worked there. Rumsfeld felt the Pentagon walls shake and left his office to help with the rescue until taken away to safety.[3]

Minutes after the Pentagon was hit, Vice President Richard Cheney phoned President George W. Bush on *Air Force One* and urged him not to return to Washington, D.C. The White House had received a threat that they would be attacked next, and the staff feared for the president's safety.[4] Not since the British burned the White House in 1814 during the War of 1812 (1812–1815) had a president been persuaded by security concerns to avoid the Capitol.

As the president's jet zigzagged across America, George W. Bush kept in constant contact by phone of the developing tragedy on the ground. Within an hour of the World Trade Center being hit, its two towers collapsed and killed nearly three thousand people. Some of the victims included hundreds of fire and emergency rescue workers and police officers. President Bush spoke to the governor of New York, George Pataki. He expressed his grief, "I know your heart is broken."[5]

Meanwhile, there was a fourth hijacked plane. United Flight 93 took off from Newark, New Jersey, and was meant to land in San Francisco. In a series of cellular phone calls to wives, two passengers were told of the Trade Center crashes. The men told their wives that they were also being hijacked and that some of the passengers were discussing how they might stop them. Another passenger called 911 and described the hijacking in progress. Later, investigators said that they heard voices of a struggle in the cockpit. At 10:06 A.M., United Flight 93 slammed into a field about eighty miles east of Pittsburgh.[6]

Many people believe that hijacked Flight 93 was intended to hit the nation's Capitol Building or the White House.

In Washington, D.C., other White House officials and congressmen were taken to secure positions. Vice President Cheney and National Security Adviser Rice relocated their operations to a protected bunker under the White House.

A police-escorted motorcade drove the president's wife, Laura Bush, House Speaker Dennis Hastert, Democratic Leader Thomas Daschle, and Republican Leader Trent Lott to secure places away from the Capitol. Bush's twin daughters, Jenna and Barbara, at universities in Texas and Connecticut, were also taken to safety.

At 3:30 P.M., the president's jet touched down at Offutt Air Force Base in Omaha, Nebraska. George W. Bush held the first meeting of the National Security Council to discuss the terrorist crisis. The president's men knew with near certainty that Osama bin Laden, Middle Eastern leader of a terrorist organization known as al Qaeda, was behind the morning's attacks. There were three known al Qaeda organizers on American Airlines Flight 77 that had hit the Pentagon.

Al Qaeda was the only terrorist organization capable of such spectacular, well-coordinated attacks.[7]

By 4:30 P.M., George W. Bush was on *Air Force One* again. He told his Secret Service director, Brian L. Stafford, that he was heading back to the White House even though Stafford said that the Secret Service could not guarantee the president's safety.[8]

At 8:30 that night, President Bush stood in the Oval Office of the White House. In a seven-minute speech, he addressed the nation and the world. He reassured everyone of his determination to go after the terrorists.

George W. Bush said, "Today our nation saw evil." He declared that he would "make no distinction between the terrorists who committed these acts and those who harbor them."[9]

Many leaders from around the world voiced their support of President Bush while also expressing sadness for the tragedy. England's prime minister, Tony Blair, said, "This mass terrorism is the new evil in our world today."[10]

In contrast, Iraq declared that the United States deserved the attacks because of its "crimes against humanity." Iraq blamed the United States for punishing their country with sanctions after Iraq's 1990 invasion of Kuwait.

In less than twelve hours, George W. Bush's presidency had changed forever. Disputes over Social Security and testing in schools were replaced by debates

SOURCE DOCUMENT

THE PRESIDENT: Ladies and gentlemen, this is a difficult moment for America. I, unfortunately, will be going back to Washington after my remarks. Secretary Rod Paige and the Lt. Governor will take the podium and discuss education. I do want to thank the folks here at Booker Elementary School for their hospitality.

Today we've had a national tragedy. Two airplanes have crashed into the World Trade Center in an apparent terrorist attack on our country. I have spoken to the Vice President, to the Governor of New York, to the Director of the FBI, and have ordered that the full resources of the federal government go to help the victims and their families, and to conduct a full-scale investigation to hunt down and to find those folks who committed this act.

Terrorism against our nation will not stand.

And now if you would join me in a moment of silence. May God bless the victims, their families, and America. Thank you very much.

At 9:30 A.M. on September 11, 2001, President Bush spoke to the nation stating, "Today we've had a national tragedy."

on how America should combat terrorism and whether the country should go to war.

Throughout his life, George W. Bush had been compared to his father, the forty-first president of the United States, George H. W. Bush. Some critics said that young Bush accomplished little on his own. They said he had gotten into the best schools, became successful in the oil business, and had even gotten his start in politics because he was the son of George H. W. Bush and possessed the powerful Bush name.

On September 11, 2001, George W. Bush stood alone. George Walker Bush, forty-third president of the United States, prepared to lead the country through this crisis and into the future. He was about to make some of the most important decisions in his nation's history. And he was ready to do it his own way.

2

GROWING UP IN
TEXAS AND NEW
ENGLAND

George Walker Bush was born on July 6, 1946, in New Haven, Connecticut. His parents are George Herbert Walker Bush and Barbara Pierce Bush.

The first Bush son was named after his father, George. His middle name, Walker, was his grandmother Bush's maiden name. The family did not want Junior or II attached to the end of his name. Instead, George W. was called "Little George" or "Georgie."[1]

Little George Bush received a lot of love and influence from his family. He had been born into a very powerful and rich New England family. Their roots represented years of political and social leadership.

George W.'s grandfather, Prescott Bush, was a man with a very deep voice who stood over six feet tall and

George W. Bush was born on July 6, 1946, to Barbara and George Herbert Walker Bush.

weighed nearly 250 pounds. He was a U.S. senator from Connecticut. He also served as a member of the governing boards at Yale University, the Prudential Insurance Company, the Pan Am Air Company, CBS, and Dresser Industries. When Prescott Bush died at seventy-seven of lung cancer, his grandson George W., in his mid-twenties, missed him, seeing him as a living treasure, a living legacy.[2]

George W. shared leadership traits from his mother's family as well. His mother's father, Marvin Pierce, was president of the McCall Publishing Company and a descendant of the fourteenth president of the United States, Franklin Pierce.[3]

George W.'s grandparents provided love and models of leadership. But his greatest influence came from his parents.

His mother, Barbara Pierce, had been a debutante, a socialite, in her youth. In 1941, at sixteen, Barbara was at home in New York, on a school break from Ashley Hall, a private school in South Carolina. At a Christmas party in Greenwich, Connecticut, she met her future husband, George H. W. Bush.

George H. W. was a high school senior at the elite Phillips Academy in Massachusetts. Awkward at dancing and shy, he asked a friend, Jack Wozencraft, to introduce him to Barbara Pierce. She was impressed by George H. W., and they began dating. They were officially engaged two years later. They married the following year in January 1945.[4] Another year and a half later, they became the proud parents of son George W.

George W.'s father would become a living legacy for the first son. In many ways, George W. would spend his life following in his father's footsteps.[5] George W. could not help but be influenced by the life of his very remarkable father.

At eighteen, George W.'s father enlisted in the Navy and entered pilot school where he became the youngest commissioned fighter pilot at the time.[6] He flew fifty-eight missions and survived being shot down by the Japanese. For his bravery and mission experiences, George Herbert Walker Bush received the Distinguished Flying Cross.[7] The medal is awarded to those who perform heroic or extraordinary achievement while on flying operations. He was a genuine hero.

George H. W. entered Yale University, the same university attended by his father, uncle, and older brother. He majored in economics. He did charity work as a part of his membership in the Delta Kappa Epsilon fraternity, and he was also a part of the elite secret society of Skull and Bones.

After graduating from Yale in 1948, George H. W. Bush could have stayed in New England and followed the powerful path of the Walker, Bush, and Pierce fame. But he wanted to make his own money in a very risky and untried way. When George W. was nearly two, father George H. W. pulled up their comfortable family

George H. W. Bush (center) enlisted in the Navy and became the youngest commissioned fighter pilot at the time.

roots in Connecticut and moved to the dusty, dirty, dry plains of Texas. He hoped to make it big in the oil industry, a business venture that was just getting re-established at the time in Texas after the Depression.

The change could not have been more drastic. From a roomy home in lush New England, the young Bush family rented a one-bedroom duplex apartment on a tiny, fifty-foot lot. They owned the only refrigerator on the block and shared a bathroom with another couple. Odessa was a barren Texas town where "the clouds on bad days sometimes looked like dirty, airborne ashtrays." Often the air would be "sluggish, thick with the bitter smell of oil."[8]

The Bushes later moved into their first house in Midland, Texas. Their housing development was called Easter Egg Row because the houses looked like dyed eggs in a carton. Each one was painted a different pastel color. The Bushes' two-bedroom house was a light blue. George W.'s first childhood friend Randall "Randy" Roden called the development the "ugliest place on the face of the earth."[9]

In Midland, little George W. would become the oldest brother to the rest of the Bush family that eventually included Robin, Jeb, Marvin, Neil, and Dorothy.

To be successful, George W.'s father was on the road or in the office most of the time. Barbara had her hands full taking care of the home and the Bush children. The job was not easy. She recalled, the "diapers, runny noses, earaches, more Little League games than you can believe possible. . . ." Some times were so low that she had the feeling that "I'd never have fun again," she said.[10]

During the early years, George W.'s mother was his biggest influence. He owes his own outspoken and witty nature to her. He said, "My mother [is] very outspoken [and] lets it rip if she's got something on her mind. Once it's over, you know exactly where you stand and that's it."[11]

The love of George W.'s parents became even stronger after three-year-old Robin died. Robin, the second child and first daughter, had leukemia. Several medical trips locally and back East to various doctors and hospitals could not save her. Her death hit seven-year-old George W. especially hard.

George W. was in school on the day Robin died in October 1953. When his parents picked him up from his second-grade class, the news shattered him. He knew Robin was sick, but he had no idea she was dying. Years later, he explained, "You think your life is so good and everything is perfect; then something like this happens and nothing is the same."[12]

Among the five Bush children, "Georgie" stood out as the leader. Neil Bush said that his big brother George W. "was as close to being the boss as you could be. I mean . . . they looked up to him and respected him and were . . . maybe . . . a little afraid of him from time to time."[13]

Brother Marvin said, "In our house, you can count

on George to liven things up." He was always throwing down challenges, telling his brothers to suck it up as he passed them out on the jogging track. Even at the dinner table, George was the blustery, nonstop, sharp-elbowed, always digging one—the one who, when his mother looked away, would make a face.[14]

George W. was a leader in the neighborhood as well. He got the neighbor boys on bicycles, and they would patrol the tiny city of Midland. Everyone knew him.

He also knew everyone—by name. It was a talent he inherited from his grandfather, Prescott Bush. In the early 1900s, Prescott dazzled his classmates with his amazing ability to memorize names.[15] George W. was even better at it. Whether there were ten, twenty, or hundreds of names, he could recite them all minutes after meeting them. And the people were pleased that he could remember.

George W. never forgot a baseball stat or a lineup either. He owned valuable Yankee cards but was a big New York Giants fan. He pasted Topps baseball cards to postcards and mailed them to players in spring training. He hoped to get their autographs when they mailed them back, and he often did.

George H. W. Bush's oil business was a success. In 1955, the Bush family moved from their small home in Midland to a 3,000-square-foot house in Houston, Texas. It had a swimming pool and was next to a park.

In Houston, George H. W. Bush was closer to big city politics. He had been building membership in the Texas

Republican Party ever since the Bushes moved to Texas. The state had traditionally been a Democratic one. The growing oil industry had attracted a lot of easterners who brought their Republican Party beliefs with them. George H. W. was becoming recognized as a primary Republican Party leader.

When the family moved to Houston, George W.'s life became one of more money and privilege. He was enrolled in Kinkaid, a very exclusive, private junior high school. Some of the changes from his public school days in Midland shocked him. He said, "One day at Kinkaid a guy walks up to me after practice and says, 'Hey, you want a ride home, Bush?' . . . This was an eighth grader, who may have been fourteen at the time, and driving a GTO [a high-performance car from Pontiac]—in the eighth grade! . . . It was just a different world!"[16]

George W. realized that he, too, was different from other kids because of his family's success in oil and of his father's political activities. He was aware that people expected him to be a lot like his father. They believed that he would easily step into his dad's oil business when he grew of age.[17]

But his father said that there was no pressure. "Barbara and I never tried to put any pressure on our five kids to be something they didn't want to be. . . . I would hope we've tried to say to George, 'look, be what you want to be, and don't let them fit you into a mold where everybody's got to be exactly alike.'"[18]

After George W. ended his eighth-grade year, he

faced moving from Texas to New England in order to continue his education at Phillips Academy in Andover, Massachusetts. George W.'s father and grandfather had attended Phillips, and it was still one of the most exclusive schools in the country.

Although he had never left home before, son George said he was "game" to try Massachusetts and began his four years starting in autumn 1961.

At Phillips Academy, George W. faced his father's schoolboy reputation. Before he graduated in 1942, George H. W. had earned twenty-three class distinctions. His honors included president of the senior class, chair of student deacons, and captains of both varsity soccer and basketball teams.

George W. had to adjust to major differences between his Texas school and the Massachusetts academy. Phillips was obsessed with academic competition. Classes were harder than anything George W. had taken before, and he barely earned average grades. Another surprise were the cold winters where he experienced snow for the first time. In addition, George W. was used to girls being a part of his classes, but Phillips was an all-boys school. No one was permitted to even exchange letters, let alone talk to, the girls who attended nearby Abbott School for Girls.[19]

But George W. adjusted and made his own way at Phillips. He knew he was not good enough to be in the academic or athletic spotlight, but he did not want to be left out. Instead, George chose to be "cool." He was a "cutup" and a socializer.[20] He talked and teased with everyone, both inside and outside of his own group of friends.

George W. excelled at being head cheerleader. In an academy of all boys, sports were as important as classes, and cheerleading was a much-desired position. There was nothing feminine about screaming your lungs out for ol' Blue and White. In fact, there was competition to be on the squad.[21] Classmates fed off of George W.'s energy whenever he led his eight-man squad, each carrying a megaphone, out to the football games.

In 1964, when George W. graduated from the academy, he was named BMOC, or Big Man on Campus, in the yearbook. Later, his classmates remembered him most for bringing fun back to the academically serious institution. When he returned years later to a Phillips reunion, George W. had to confess. He said that he had been terrified of failure, since this was the institution so beloved by his father.[22]

George W. continued in his father's footsteps when he began college at Yale University in the fall of 1964. Although his father and grandfather both graduated from Yale, George W. was not sure if his grades were good enough to get him accepted. At the time, his grandfather served on Yale's board of trustees. Because of his grandfather's close ties with the university, "it was simply assumed that George W. was eventually going to be admitted."[23] And he was. Today, though, George W. maintains that he was accepted on his own merits.

George W. Bush continued in his father's footsteps when he began college at Yale University in 1964.

There were three months of summer before George W. began college. Back in Houston, he joined his father's first, full-time campaign trail. George H. W. Bush was running for the chair of the Harris County Republican Party.

As the Bush election team crossed the Texas prairies and plains, sometimes George W. reluctantly stepped to the front of the stage in support of his father. By fall, George W. had to quit the campaign and head once again to the East, this time to New Haven, Connecticut.

Like at Phillips, George W.'s father had been remembered as a model student and an athlete at Yale University. Nearly every wall and display case held photos, newspaper clippings, and trophies that spoke of George H. W. Bush's excellence in sports, fraternities, and service organizations when he attended in the late 1940s.

George W. again struggled to make decent grades but continued to excel at socializing. As soon as he arrived, George W. began making friends. While his two roommates divided the space in the dorm room, freshman Bush was out the door meeting people. Within three to four days, a big percentage of the campus knew who he was.

Later, George W. Bush admitted, "I was never a great intellectual."[24] So he got involved in other ways. He joined Delta Kappa Epsilon fraternity, or DKE. It was a fraternity of male athletes that his father had once joined. George W.'s amazing ability to memorize names quickly got him noticed. At one initiation party, George W., along with a few other freshmen, was ordered to name as many people in the room as possible. The others could recall only four or five. George W., one by one, named all fifty-four people in the room. Everyone was floored.[25]

The fraternity became the center of his college life. According to Edgar Cullman, a college classmate, Bush was "always in the middle of things, whatever group activity was going on, whatever pranks might be going on. He had natural leadership. He wasn't afraid to look foolish. He didn't care."[26] Bush's top three interests at the time were sports, girls, and all-night poker games. George W. also became a heavy drinker.

George W. joined the secret Skull and Bones society that was known for its activities that imitated death. Although Yale had seven other secret groups, only the wealthiest young men from the most powerful families were chosen members in the Skull and Bones.

Meetings of the Skull and Bones are held in a triple-padlocked, windowless mausoleum. Inside are faded, dark portraits of former members called Bonesmen. Walls are covered with dark, red velvet. Shelves and tabletops are adorned with skulls and bones. Some of the group's mysterious reputation comes from its special nods, coded numbers, and secret names.

George W.'s membership in the Skull and Bones, his drinking, and his suspected drug usage would raise questions and create negative publicity thirty years later during his run for president.

Yale University provided George W. Bush with a vast network of male friends. They would help him in politics and in business throughout his life. He stayed buddies with his sports clubs and the brothers from DKE. But some of his closest friends were those from Skull and Bones.[27]

One issue that bothered George W. during his college years involved the Vietnam War. The Vietnam War, a conflict dealing with communism, split the Asian country into North and South Vietnam. The war began around 1954. The United States became involved in the war in the 1960s when it feared that communism would spread throughout the eastern region. Communism went against the beliefs of American democracy and capitalism. As the war continued, the government sent more and more American soldiers into Vietnam.

On Yale's campus, some students took part in debates and protests against the government's decision to continue fighting the war. George W. was silent on the war discussion, although he was pro-military and proud of his father's service in World War II.

George W. Bush graduated from Yale in 1968 with a history degree. According to the military Selective Service Act, as soon as George W. received his college diploma, he could be required to enter the military.

He wondered: Would the government draft him or should he enlist in the military on his own? Would he be sent to Vietnam? The questions were being asked by millions of men his age.

The Selective Service Act of 1940 states that all eighteen-year-old males must register with the Selective Service System. The registered men can be drafted or ordered to serve, if a crisis occurs that requires more troops than the voluntary military can supply. In 1965, President Lyndon Johnson called on all registered men to prepare for military service to help fight the war in Vietnam.

The Selective Service Act included about eight categories, or classifications, that exempted men from service. One classification was for college men. For George W. and his male classmates, that exemption ended as soon as they graduated. Many talked about their options.

To avoid being a soldier, they could break the law. They could escape to another country like Canada and escape the draft. They could hurt themselves severely enough to be declared physically unable to serve. They could claim to be conscientious objectors and argue that war was against their belief system. They could hope for a military position that kept them in the states rather than sent them overseas.

George W. took the last option. He said, "I was not prepared to shoot my eardrum out with a shotgun in order to get a deferment. Nor was I willing to go to Canada. I decided to better myself by learning how to fly airplanes."[28] Twelve days before his college graduation, George W. enlisted with the Texas Air National Guard.

In spite of waiting lists and poor test scores, George W. was accepted immediately into the Texas Air National Guard unit.[29]

His stateside enlistment would become an issue of disagreement during his presidential campaign. His opponents would say that only because of his father's "pull" was George W. accepted in the National Guard and able to avoid Vietnam.

Bush's opponents would also argue that there was a waiting list of five hundred men, and George W. barely passed the entrance aptitude test for pilots. They would also argue that the National Guard officials showed favoritism because they knew George W.'s father was a congressman who supported the war.

George W. insisted he was not trying to avoid fighting. He wanted to be an Air Force pilot like his father. If ordered, George W. said, he would have gone to Vietnam.[30]

After two years of flight training in Texas, George W. graduated with his National Guard wings. During the next four years, he was obligated to part-time service, one weekend a month, in the Guard.

Once out of Guard training, George W. headed to Florida. He transferred his monthly duties to the Florida National Guard. He relocated to help his father's political friend, Edward Gurney. Gurney sought a Republican victory in Florida. His election win to the U.S. Senate

In 1965, during the Vietnam War, men could be drafted to fight in the conflict overseas. In order not to be drafted, George W. Bush enlisted with the Texas Air National Guard.

was historic. Florida had traditionally been a Democratic state, but Gurney was a fierce campaigner.

Working with Edward Gurney taught George W. about the "power of a more conservative candidate than his father."[31] The experience gave twenty-year-old George W. some valuable lessons when he began his own run for political office.

After the campaign, George W. finally went home to Texas. He had no idea what to do next. He turned to his father for help.

3

EARLY POLITICAL MOVES

In 1972, George H. W. Bush arranged for his son to work at Project PULL, an antipoverty program in Houston's inner-city wards. In these poor, crowded areas of the city, George W. worked as an assistant to John White and as a counselor to kids. He took them on outings and sometimes visited their schools—a new world to him.

George W. grew very close to an unruly, tough kindergartner named Jimmy. The two were inseparable. If Jimmy arrived shirtless and shoeless, George W. took him out for new clothes.

Years later, President George W. Bush remembered his experience at PULL. "It was very meaningful for me because it gave me a chance to interface with kids that I never would have known. Years later, when John White told me that Jimmy had been shot, it broke my heart."[1]

Leaving the PULL program, George W. was not sure what he wanted to do. He considered running for the Texas legislature, and his decision was briefly mentioned in the paper. Ultimately, he decided against it. Not having held a job for longer than a year was a disadvantage.

George W. worked on another Republican campaign. He was the political director for Winton M. "Red" Blount. Blount ran for a U.S. Senate seat in Alabama against a Democrat with thirty-six years of political experience. Though Blount fought hard, he had no charisma and lost in the 1972 election. During this experience, George W. picked up another valuable lesson: A candidate had to either make friends with the voters or face defeat.[2]

George W. enjoyed his campaign experiences. His uncle, Jonathan Bush, told the *Washington Post* newspaper that he was sure his nephew was going to become a political consultant.[3] George W., however, decided to go back to school.

In 1973, he was rejected by the University of Texas but accepted into Harvard University Business School. For the third time, George W. reluctantly left Texas and headed east to Massachusetts. He planned to earn a master's degree in business.

Although he reunited with old friends from Phillips Academy and Yale, George W. did not like the intellectual atmosphere. Always wearing his National Guard flight jacket, "he talked constantly about Texas and chewed tobacco."[4] He spent his weekends with relatives in New York, Maine, and Connecticut. He played some intramural sports and visited nightclubs.

While George W. attended Harvard, his father, who had risen to higher levels in the Republican Party, now more than ever, was the subject of many campus political debates.

The source of the debates centered on a historic "break-in" that originally occurred in 1972. Called the Watergate scandal, it involved some top level Republicans from President Richard Nixon's staff who planned a burglary at the Watergate Hotel in Washington, D.C., that was then the national headquarters of the Democratic Party. The men were caught, and President Nixon was questioned regarding his role in the break-in. Nixon denied any involvement. Government investigations continued to search for all those responsible.

Meanwhile, President Nixon's vice president, Spiro Agnew, was the focus of another investigation. In 1973, Agnew was found guilty of bribery and extortion when he was a county executive and governor of Maryland, before his vice presidency. On October 10, Spiro Agnew resigned from office as the vice president. Two days later, Nixon asked the Senate to confirm Gerald Ford as the new vice president, the first appointed vice president in United States history.

A year later, in 1974, government investigations determined that President Nixon knew about the Watergate burglary and had tried to keep his involvement a secret from the investigators. Rather than face an impeachment trial that could lead toward his forced removal from office, Richard Nixon resigned as president on August 9.

Vice President Gerald Ford took over as president. The question now was: Who would serve as vice president? The choices were Nelson D. Rockefeller and George H. W. Bush. In the end, Ford chose Rockefeller.

George W. graduated from business school in 1975 and was twenty-nine years old. He could have applied for jobs at successful companies in New York. At least 65 percent of Harvard graduates headed to these large corporations. But George W. told his friends and relatives that it was time for him to leave the East. "West Texas is a doer environment," he explained. "People can do things."[5]

His mother said, "Harvard was a great turning point for him."[6] George W. had a new focus and a desire to start his own oil company. He returned to the city of his boyhood, Midland, Texas.

Using his father's successful reputation in business and politics, George W. called on family, friends, and acquaintances. He received a lot of advice and financial help from them. They returned his phone calls as a matter of both loyalty and obligation.[7]

Even with help, George W. would not be an immediate success because the oil industry had changed a lot in the twenty years since his father entered it.

By the 1970s, an oilman saw a loss in oil profits,

a loud call for environmental protection, and price controls. Whereas, in 1953, it was easy to get the land rights for oil drilling. It seemed wherever the drill entered the ground, it found a successful oil flow.

George W. soon incorporated his own oil company. He called it Arbusto, which is Spanish for "bush." It became marginally successful. The company's secretary, Kim Dyches, believed that George W. enjoyed raising money for the company more than securing land deals or running any other aspect of the business. "I'm sure he was somewhat charismatic, and name recognition and all the ties made it easier for him," she said.[8]

George W. gained a reputation. Some oilmen friends nicknamed him "The Bombastic Bushkin." It referred to his being a "foul-mouthed cut-up who was trying hard to be one of the natives." He became quite a drinker. His father cautioned him to "lay off the drinking and take care of his fledgling career."[9]

He was also cheap. His clothes were either old or borrowed. He wore hand-me-down sharkskin shoes that his uncle, Jonathan Bush, had given him. He Scotch-taped the tassels on his loafer shoes when they fell off. At his apartment, he lashed his broken bed frame together with neckties. His good friend Charlie Younger said, "The buffalo [nickel] would squeal when it left his hand."[10]

In 1977, after two years back in Texas, George W. decided to run for the Nineteenth Congressional District. His decision surprised a lot of people even,

Like his father, George W. Bush wanted to get into the oil business. He started his own business with the advice and help of family friends and acquaintances.

though they knew him as a person who was quick to act on ideas and schemes as soon as they popped into his head. His friends agreed that George W. certainly had experience in political campaigns, but they did not think he could be a political candidate himself.

"We were saying: Why do you want to do this?" explained his friend Joe O'Neill. "He looked around . . . and said, 'Are you gonna do it?' . . . He said, 'Well then, I am.'"[11]

While on the campaign trail, George W. decided to get married. His decision was a shock to some of his friends. George W. enjoyed the company of popular young women who had as much energy to have fun as he did. He dated often and had once been engaged to a socialite while he attended Yale. It therefore surprised some of his friends when he became quite serious with Laura Welch, who was not like the young women he dated. Laura was a very quiet, disciplined woman.

Laura Welch was once an elementary teacher but now worked as a children's librarian. George W. and Laura met at a barbecue hosted by mutual friends. No one expected the two would get along. "Laura was more ladylike . . . and George was more the rambunctious reveler and a rambler," described a friend.[12]

Laura said the thing she liked about George W. was "he made me laugh." George W. said, "I found her to be very thoughtful, smart, interested person—one of the great listeners. And since I'm one of the big talkers, it was a great fit."[13]

George W. Bush and Laura Welch were married on November 5, 1977.

On November 5, 1977, three months after meeting, they married at the United Methodist Church in Midland. It was a simple wedding with seventy guests. The Bushes spent a day or so in Mexico for a quick honeymoon. Then George W. was back on his campaign trail.

George W. loved the political campaign. He walked neighborhoods with the hot sun beating down on him. He knocked on more than sixty-five doors a day. If no one was home, he'd leave a hand-written note, like his father had taught him. Robert Birge, George W.'s friend from Skull and Bones, explained, "I've always admired his ability to interact with people and his effectiveness in getting his point across."[14]

But his Democratic opponent, Kent Hance, painted George W. Bush as an "outsider." He said that George W. had been born in New England and spent many years in school there. Bush did not know what a real Texan wanted and needed. Hance was a better debater than Bush.[15] Also, Hance easily angered George W. Bush when he attacked the political decisions made by Bush's father.

George W. said, "When it comes to the integrity of my father, I will fight back. They are trying to slam me by slamming my father."[16]

George W. lost the election, with 47 percent voting for him and 53 percent for his opponent. He learned lessons that he probably knew were true all along. He learned he had to rally support and make people feel comfortable and happy. Next time, he would make sure that he had a solid background to run on and an easy-going manner to please the voters.[17]

While George W. was trying to get elected to Congress, George H. W. had made a run for the presidency. However, in a bitter primary runoff, Ronald Reagan, who once had been a movie star and a governor of California, had soundly beaten George H. W. Bush for the Republican Party's presidential nomination.

Although crushed by Reagan's own desire to be president, George H. W. accepted when Ronald Reagan asked him to be his running mate for vice president. In 1980, Ronald Reagan was elected the nation's leader.

In 1977, George W. Bush decided to run for Congress. This campaign flyer shows Bush with his wife, Laura.

With his own campaign over and his father the vice president of the United States, George W. focused on his own affairs. He and Laura wanted children, which meant that he needed a steadier income.

George W. concentrated on making his oil company, Arbusto, successful until he found a buyer for it.

In early summer of 1981, Laura Bush learned that she was pregnant with twins. On November 25, 1981, Jenna and Barbara, named after their grandmothers, were born. New father George W. was elated. He said that their birth was the most thrilling moment of his life.[18]

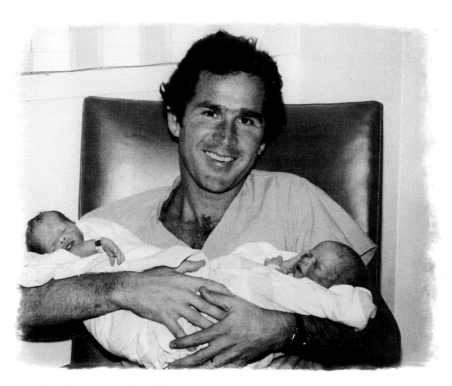

On November 25, 1981, George W. and Laura Bush became the proud parents of twin girls, Jenna and Barbara.

George W. was able to sell part of his oil company. It was renamed Bush Exploration. In 1986, the Harken Energy Corporation bought out Bush Exploration. Although he no longer owned it, George W. was hired as a Harken board member and consultant.

A desire for politics and a request by his father soon called George W. back to the campaign trial. President Ronald Reagan's maximum two terms were ending in 1988. Vice President George H. W. Bush prepared to run for president. He selected Lee Atwater to head his presidential campaign. George H. W. wanted his son to be a senior adviser on his election campaign. The experience would not only encourage George W. to run for his own office, it would also give him the knowledge to win it.

However, before he became too active in his father's campaign, George W. made two very personal, life-changing decisions. The first one was quitting a long-standing drinking habit, and the second was leaving Midland, Texas.

Drinking alcohol had become a daily custom for George W. since his fraternity days at Yale. His father and his wife had cautioned him about his excessiveness. Laura said it was necessary to stop.[19] George W. found the courage to quit. Two things motivated him. One was the words of a religious leader. The second was his image as his father's political adviser.

George W. met the well-known religious evangelist Billy Graham in Maine. The Reverend Billy Graham was a frequent guest of the Bushes at the family summer home. Graham often gave personal spiritual messages to the family. During one particular stay in 1985, said George W., Graham "planted a seed in my heart and I began to change."[20]

Preparing to work on his father's 1988 presidential campaign also convinced George W. to quit. He did not want to do anything that might be an embarrassment to his father.

The change came the day after a party. George W., his wife, and close friends attended a birthday celebration in Colorado. George W. had a lot to drink. When he woke up the next day with a hangover, he decided to quit.

Friend Joe O'Neill explained, "He looked in the mirror and said, 'Someday, I might embarrass my father. It might get my dad in trouble.' . . . And he never took another drink."[21]

Another major change was the Bushes' move from Texas to Washington, D.C. George W. needed to be closer to his father's political campaign. After twelve years in Midland, in May 1987, George W. sold the house, packed the family wagon, and drove to the nation's capitol.

George W. was honored to serve as his father's senior political adviser. At the Republican Convention, he served as head of the Texas delegation. Standing on the floor of the convention hall, George W. called out the state's 111 votes in favor of his father. "For a man we respect and a man we love," George W. said, choking up, "for her favorite son and the best father in America . . . the man

The Bush family enjoys a game of horseshoes. George W. Bush was a senior adviser for his father's presidential run in 1988.

who made me proud every single day of my life and a man who would make America proud, the next president of the United States."[22]

As vice president, George H. W. Bush was busy in two directions. One was his job as vice president to Ronald Reagan. The second was working with his presidential campaign staff. George W. became an important figure in keeping order for his father and the election team.

George W.'s duties required him to be everywhere at once. He oversaw the Texas Republican delegation. He got the press to focus on his father, and he arranged pro-Bush crowds at hotel lobbies. He basically packaged the presidential presentation of his father.

Foremost, George W. was a bridge. He conveyed his mother's wishes to the campaign team. He conveyed his father's wishes to the growing, powerful Christian Right movement. He conveyed his father's campaign messages to the press.

During this time, a very powerful voice in the nation was gaining strength. That voice was labeled the "Christian Right." Made up of Christian conservatives, the group believed they had the power to decide an election. They felt they could convince all Christian conservatives in America to vote for their pro-Christian choice. The Republicans hoped they would choose George H. W. Bush for president.

George W. met with many supporters of the Christian Right. One person was Doug Wead. He became a strong ally and friend of the Bushes. Doug Wead came up with the phrase "compassionate conservative." George W. would use it as his personal label during his own presidential campaign years later.[23]

An equally tough job was George W.'s work with the media. George W. did not favor the press, especially the media from the Northeast. As political adviser, it was his job to convey accurately his father's political message to that very same press.[24]

The media people were aware of George W.'s dislike for them. David Hoffman, a reporter for the *Washington Post* who covered the presidency, said that George W. "disliked journalists, and I felt he was suspicious [of us]."[25]

George W. was known to have yelling matches and to have disliked the press. Once Margaret Warner, a writer for *Newsweek* magazine, referred to George W.'s father as a "wimp" seven times in her article, and the magazine cover used the word "wimp" in its title along with a poor photo of George H. W. Bush. George W. called her and chewed her out, reportedly telling her how disgraceful it was.[26]

George W. also played the role of "surrogate presidential candidate." Many times his father was away on vice presidential business for President Reagan or in another part of the campaign trail. Often George W. took over and campaigned for his father's views and held hundreds of interviews.[27]

George W. gained the reputation of being something of a "tough guy" and an "enforcer."[28] He made sure staff remained loyal and did their jobs properly. He also made many friends and connections. George W. would count on these people's support when he needed them in the future.

George W. campaigned hard for his father. He did it out of love and also because he believed in his father's political endeavors. It was not unusual when, along the campaign trail, the press asked George W. about his own political ambitions.

George W. always put down any suggestion that he was trying to prepare the way for his own political goals. When asked about his desire to run for an office, he often responded, "My horizons are limited because

I'm only interested in one George Bush political career and that's my dad's."[29]

Running against the Democratic opponent, Michael Dukakis, George H. W. Bush won the electoral vote in forty states and 53.4 percent of the popular vote. In January 1989, he was sworn in as the forty-first president of the United States.

George W.'s job as campaign adviser was over. His father was the president, holding the highest office in the land. "What's gonna happen to me?" George W. wondered aloud.[30] He had no interest in staying in D.C. Traveling across the country on behalf of his father, he had already spent too much time away from Laura and the girls.

The time seemed right to head back home to Texas and ignite once more his own political ambitions.

4

FROM BASEBALL
MANAGER TO
TEXAS GOVERNOR

George W. quickly left his father's political campaign behind. Three days after the election in mid-November 1988, George W. bought a home in Dallas, Texas, and moved his family out of Washington, D.C. He did not stop thinking about politics and about his own run for a political office.

One friend he made during his father's presidential campaign was Karl Rove from Austin. Karl Rove had worked with the Republican Party for a long time. He was a strong supporter of George W.'s own political goals. Rove suggested that George W. run for the governor of Texas in 1990. George W. disagreed.

George W. knew that he had gained a lot more political experience during the last few years by working on his friends' and his father's major political campaigns.

But he also knew that without a job and with his being out of Texas for a while, he would be at a disadvantage. The voters of Texas may not see him as one of their own.

George W. began making plans to increase his name recognition in Texas as well as earn himself a job. The plan involved one of his all-time passions: baseball.

George W. had told everyone that he grew up "wanting to be Willie Mays," the famous baseball player for the San Francisco Giants.[1] Now he dreamed of owning the Houston Astros.

While George W. was busy running his father's presidential campaign, Eddie Chiles, owner of the Texas Rangers baseball team, was ready to sell.

The price tag for the Texas Rangers was steep: $75 million for 86 percent of the team. George W. worked with then-baseball commissioner Peter Ueberroth to convince a variety of businessmen to invest collectively in the team as group owners. George W. and Ed "Rusty" Rose became general partners to the public. They would deal with the media and the public.[2]

George W. loved the position. He attended every Texas Rangers home game. Instead of sitting behind the glass windows of the special box seats, George W. sat right behind the dugout. Everyone watching the Rangers on television saw him. He created an image of being the average Texan. Although he was the son of the president of the United States, he was eating hot dogs and drinking soda, just like any other person.

George W. Bush (right) decided to buy the Texas Rangers baseball team, with other businessmen. Bush enjoyed the position as general manager. Standing with George W. is his father (left) and Joe Morgan (center), a broadcaster of baseball games.

His position as the Texas Rangers general manager had its needed effect. According to George W.'s friend and personal political adviser Karl Rove, George's work with the Texas Rangers "anchors him clearly as a Texas businessman and entrepreneur, and gives him name identification, exposure, and gives him something that will be easily recallable by people."[3]

While promoting the Texas Rangers, George W. improved his speaking skills. He also publicized his image as a good family man and a decent ordinary guy who loved Texas.

His work for the Texas team also became a good

financial move. Years later, when the owners decided to sell the Rangers, George W.'s initial investment of $606,000 earned him $14.9 million. At the time of the sale, in 1998, George W. at fifty-two had all the money he would ever need.[4]

In 1992, George W.'s father ran for reelection to a second term as president. His Democratic opponent was Governor Bill Clinton from Arkansas. Another highly

In 1992, George H. W. Bush (left) ran for reelection to a second term as president. During a televised debate, he discussed the issues with H. Ross Perot (center) and Bill Clinton (right).

publicized opponent was H. Ross Perot, who ran as a Reform Party candidate. George H. W. Bush's campaign did not run as smoothly as his first one. It seemed full of errors.

George W. did not play an active role in his father's reelection run. However, a few months before election day, George W. headed up to Washington, D.C., to work exclusively on bettering the campaign.

Once again, George W. traveled across the country, speaking for his father. His approach was a much smoother mix of politics, family values, and baseball. He seemed more fit for the politician's role than he did in 1988.[5]

In spite of George H. W.'s best efforts, as well as those of his son's and the campaign team's, George H. W. lost the 1992 presidential election to Bill Clinton.

As his father retired from his career in politics, George W. felt he was ready to run for the Texas governorship. Karl Rove was certainly behind his decision, but other friends and family still had doubts about his ability to win.

One doubt concerned the Bush name. George W. confided to a friend in Dallas his worry that Texans would never see him as a "real person." Even though he was forty years old, whenever people would hear his name, they would still simply think of his father.[6] In other ways, some voters might see the father's one term as a losing president and see son George W. as a losing candidate as well.

Another challenge was trying to win against his opponent. The state's current governor was Democrat Ann Richards, who was very well known for her homespun charm, her blue business suits, and her stylized silver hair. She had been featured in *Vogue, Vanity Fair, Glamour, Cosmopolitan, Ladies Home Journal*, and the *New York Times*. She appeared on television's *60 Minutes* and with talk show hosts Jay Leno and David Letterman. According to the polls in 1993, Ann Richards was the most popular governor in thirty years.[7]

Laura Bush expressed her hesitation about her husband entering the campaign. She preferred a quiet life at home with her community activities, her garden, and her daughters. George W. said, "She wanted to make sure that this was something I really wanted to do and that I wasn't being drug in as a result of friends, or, well, 'you're supposed to do it in order to prove yourself vis-à-vis your father.'"[8] She was not sure that she wanted to be a career politician's wife.

George W. believed he had a good shot at winning. He believed that more Texans knew who he was. "I think I can win this," he told all his friends and family.[9]

He drew up and stuck to a campaign strategy that promoted four basic issues: tort reform, education, crime, and welfare reform. Tort reform concerned reducing frivolous lawsuits. Education involved giving more local control to school districts. George W. wanted to cut crime by refusing parole to sex offenders and imposing harsher penalties on juveniles. He wanted to slash welfare rosters.[10] Bush never wavered from these four issues.

George W. had learned a lot from his past campaigns for his father's friends, for his own father, and especially from his own campaign loss. He remembered what to do and what not to do when running for a political office. George W.'s strategy against the popular opponent Ann Richards was to make himself seem "more Texan and more All-American" than she was.[11] He also vowed to himself to control his temper and extinguish any possible angry outbursts.

George W. loved campaigning, plunging into crowds, patting backs, and grabbing hands and elbows in Texas handshakes. After eighteen months, he grew more popular in the polls.

George W. did not sleep during the night before election day. He woke up very early. At his voters' polling station, he realized that he had forgotten his wallet and his voter's identification card. The election official let him vote anyway.

George W. was the winner, 53 percent to 46 percent. He had won by 334,066 votes, the biggest margin in twenty years.[12]

That night, newly elected governor George W. Bush, his wife, Laura, and the twins, Jenna and Barbara, stood on the stage at the Marriott Hotel's Capitol Ballroom in Austin. The room was crowded. It looked like half of the population of Midland, Texas, had come out to congratulate him. George W. thanked everyone for his and her support. Most importantly, he thanked his parents. "I particularly want to send my love to two Houstonians— in case you weren't sure who I was talking about, one of them has real gray hair and wears pearls."[13]

Knowing that his oldest son had always struggled with controlling his temper and his actions, his father could not help but remark about George W.'s growth and triumph. George W.'s win was "a great joy for us, seeing that flash on the [television] screen. I can't tell you the emotion I feel and the pride in the way he conducted himself," George H. W. Bush said.[14]

Soon after George W.'s acceptance speech, the Bushes made another move. This time they moved into the private, three-thousand-square-foot, second-floor quarters of the Texas Governor's Mansion.

As governor, George W. Bush could make some appointments to committees or boards. He could veto legislation. A two-thirds vote of the legislature could override the veto. The Texas legislature only meets for 140 days once every two years. George W., though, could call together a special session to address particular bills that had not yet been settled.

When his term began, Governor Bush got right to work promoting the four issues from his election campaign. Although he brought them to the Texas legislature, he did not make headway with them all.

As Texas's first lady, Laura Bush promoted her favorite projects. Her key achievement was instituting the Texas Book Festival. The celebration included book seminars and tributes to Texas authors.

The late 1990s was a good time for George W. to be governor. Texas rode the wave of prosperity experienced by all the fifty states. Everywhere in America, the economy was up and crime was down.

George W.'s popularity remained high, and he easily won reelection to a second term in 1998. He earned 69 percent of the vote. He became the first governor in Texas history to be returned for a back-to-back second term.[15]

Two major issues brought negative publicity to Governor George W. Bush. The issues concerned the death penalty and hate crimes.

In February 1998, Karla Faye Tucker, known as the "pickaxe murderer," became the first woman put to death in Texas since the Civil War.[16] While in prison, she became a "born-again" Christian. Many religious people did not believe she should be killed.

Movements such as the Christian Right and leaders such as the pope (head of the Roman Catholic Church) sent pleas to Governor George W. Bush to stop Tucker's execution. George W. refused to grant a reprieve. He said he trusted the state and national law enforcement systems that had sentenced Karla Faye Tucker to die by lethal injection.[17]

Another issue involved hate crimes. An African-American man, James Byrd, Jr. was decapitated after being tortured, chained to a truck, and dragged to his death by three white men. Critics were upset that Governor Bush did not travel to Jasper, Texas, to deal with the situation. George W. explained that while tensions were high in the city, his appearance would appear as if he was grandstanding.[18]

Legislators also wanted George W. to push for a hate-crimes bill. Forty states and the District of Columbia already enacted similar hate-crime laws. Governor George W. Bush did nothing to help pass the law.[19] He said he would prefer to enforce the laws already on the books. The bill died in the senate during the Texas legislature's 1999 session.[20]

On the national front, Bill Clinton had been elected to his second and final term as president in 1996. Almost immediately, the media and the public wondered who would run for president in 2000. Al Gore, Clinton's vice president, was certain to be a Democratic contender. Who would be the Republican candidate? Many looked to George W. for the answer.

5

A PRESIDENTIAL CONTENDER

At the beginning of his second, and last, term as the governor of Texas, George W. admitted he felt drawn to enter the presidential race. He also had some concerns about running. His two daughters, Jenna and Barbara, at seventeen, would be entering college during the 2000 presidential race. He was not sure he wanted them in the media spotlight. He also wished to complete the rest of his second term as governor.

President Clinton's personal and legal problems while in the White House helped convince Bush that the 2000 presidential race would be the best time for him to run.

About two years into his second term, President Bill Clinton was entangled in a sexual and legal scandal involving a White House intern named Monica

Lewinsky. Clinton faced impeachment and possible removal from office. George W.'s supporters believed that he would be the Republican who could "help lift the national moral climate."[1]

But what of George W.'s own involvement with drinking and suspected drug use? He, too, could be accused of behaving badly. George W. Bush said his own wild antics occurred when he was much younger. He would not discuss them because they existed in the past.

George W. told a reporter, "It doesn't do any good to inventory the mistakes I made when I was young. . . . when I was young and irresponsible, I was young and irresponsible. I changed when I married my wife and I changed when I had children."[2]

George W. also considered the famous Bush legacy. George W.'s last name was still his biggest advantage and biggest handicap.[3] His father had been out of politics for over five years. Perhaps now the public would see George W. as an individual, not as the forty-first president's son.

In the end, George W. felt the name issue just did not matter. "It's hard to believe," said Bush to a reporter, "but—I don't have time to worry about being George Bush's son. Maybe it's a result of being confident. I'm not sure how the psychoanalysts would analyze it, but I'm not worried about it. I'm really not. I'm a free guy."[4]

On June 12, 1999, in an airport in Cedar Rapids, Iowa, George W. Bush officially announced his bid for

Bill Clinton became entangled in scandals two years into his second term. These legal issues convinced George W. Bush to run for president of the United States.

the presidency. "I'm ready. I believe you can expect someone named George W. to win this nomination."[5]

Money began flowing into George W.'s presidential campaign fund. He attended fund-raisers and campaign events throughout the country. In the end, he would make history by collecting $37 million in the first six months of his campaign for the Republican presidential nomination.[6] The amount was nearly ten times as much money as his closest Republican rival had collected.[7] By the end of 1999, Bush would raise over $67 million.

With a maximum of a thousand dollars allowed per an individual's campaign donation, much of the money going to a Republican candidate went to George W. Bush. His opponents, who included Elizabeth Dole, Pat Buchanan, Steve Forbes, and Dan Quayle, struggled to raise the money to keep their campaigns running.[8]

Another major opponent in the run with Bush for the Republican nomination was Senator John McCain from Arizona. He and Bush disagreed over campaign finance reform, which would limit some of the amount of money political candidates received. George W. Bush said, "It's bad for Republicans and it's going to hurt the conservative cause."[9] They also argued over taxes. Bush supported a tax cut; McCain believed a tax cut would use up federal money from Social Security.

For a while, John McCain held a commanding lead in winning states' votes for the Republican presidential candidate. At one point, however, he became dismayed at what he saw as the Bush campaign's use of very negative advertising. The ads against McCain were personal as well as political.[10] In public, McCain said that he was going to pull his negative advertising and asked that Bush do the same. Bush resolved not to.[11]

As Bush rode ahead and won more and more states' primary votes, John McCain dropped out of the race and admitted defeat to George W. Bush. In March 2000, McCain endorsed Bush as the Republican choice for president.[12]

Because of Bush's soaring popularity and the amount of money in his campaign fund, George W. led the Republican field of contenders for the presidential nomination and was the favorite to win.

George W. attended the Republican Convention in Philadelphia, Pennsylvania, in August 2000. The delegates overwhelmingly chose George W. to be their candidate for president. He was officially running against Democratic vice president Al Gore.

George W. called himself a "compassionate conservative." He explained, "We are the world's only remaining superpower, and we must use our power in a strong but compassionate way to help keep the peace and encourage the spread of freedom."[13]

When the presidential debates aired on television, many people felt that Al Gore would be the better debater. He had many more years of political experience than George W. Bush. However, the public said Bush spoke better than Gore during the first two debates.

After the third and final debate, though, viewers believed both candidates did equally well.[14]

Numbers grew more and more important as the campaign reached its conclusion. During the final weeks, neither candidate gained a significant advantage. Surveys showed Bush and Gore almost dead even.

As the race took Bush and Gore from coast to coast, states that had not been important in recent elections suddenly became crucial to the outcome. Confident, George W. Bush pushed on. "I'll be the most surprised man in America if I don't win," he told Wisconsin Governor Tommy Thompson.[15]

Ten days before the election, George W. predicted he would win Michigan's eighteen and Tennessee's eleven electoral votes. He was nervous about Pennsylvania, but believed he could win Florida.

He even went after the "long shots." These were the states that usually voted for the Democrat. George W. believed that "undecided voters could be moved at the end of the campaign by the appearance of momentum" of the race.[16] Those unsure voters may turn into votes for him.

As the presidential campaign wound down to its final three weeks, the two major contenders were almost tied in the polls. Republican Bush with 48 percent had a slight edge over Democrat Gore's 44 percent.

In spite of the intensity of the campaign, George W. stuck with some of his personal habits. He insisted on returning home from the campaign most weekends. He wanted to sleep in his own bed and play with his pets. He even kept his campaign days relatively short, often finishing the last speech by 7:00 or 9:00 at night.

On the eve of election day, George W. Bush went to bed believing he had run the better campaign. He believed the people got the message that he was the best man to run the country. In just a few hours, Americans would go to the polls and decide whether Bush was right or not.

The weather dawned overcast and gloomy at the Governor's Mansion in Austin, Texas. Governor George W. Bush awoke at 6:30 A.M. and followed his personal election-day routine. He fed the pets, brewed his coffee, and read from the Bible. He posed for photographers. He accompanied his wife to the Travis County Courthouse and voted. Later, he made a few get-out-the-vote phone calls from his office.

Still early in the day, he drove to the gym at the University of Texas to work out. In spite of the campaign pressure, George W. Bush's mood was upbeat. He was confident as he awaited nationwide voting results. He believed he would be elected the forty-third president of the United States.

Bush was stunned when, while exercising, he got a call from his staff. Voting results were not good. By 2:00 in the afternoon, early returns read Bush with 49 percent of the popular vote and Gore with 48 percent overall. In Florida, Bush had 47 percent of the vote and Gore had 50 percent.

Where was the big win that George W. Bush had predicted? In state after state, the exit polls showed a closer contest than Bush had been led to believe—the projections of a fairly comfortable Republican win were falling to pieces.[17]

By 8:00 P.M. that night, Bush's confidence wavered. He admitted, "I got the smell"—the smell of defeat.[18] Then it was over. He heard and saw the television announcers proclaim his Democratic opponent Al Gore the presidential winner.

But something was wrong. The actual vote counts did not match up to the voting projections broadcasted by the news media. Could it be that the media had "jumped the gun" in order to be the first to report a winner? Two hours later, at 10:15 P.M., it certainly appeared that they had misjudged the election outcome.

Bush's confidence returned. Florida was the deciding state; whichever candidate won Florida would also win the presidency. Television networks reversed their claims. Florida's results were too close to call.

Around 2:15 the next morning, the news media declared George W. Bush the winner. Al Gore officially phoned George W. and told him the presidential race was over and George W. Bush had won.

Gore reversed his decision about an hour later when Florida tallies showed Bush with 2,909,135 votes and Gore with 2,907,351 votes. Bush's lead was an extremely slim 1,784 votes. It set the closest margin in presidential voting history.[19]

Because the lead was less than one half of one percent, by state law, an automatic recount of Florida's votes began. At this point, neither candidate could be declared a winner. The deadlock in Florida was an almost unimaginable fluke, like tossing a quarter and having it come to rest on its edge.[20]

George W. Bush's drive for the presidency was not over. For thirty-six more days, he continued to work, not with the American voters this time, but with the electoral, legal, and judicial systems.

The slim presidential margin brought to the public's awareness the Constitutional laws that govern the electing of a president. In particular, the public focused first on the Constitution's Electoral College system.

Although senators and members of the House of Representatives are elected by the popular votes of the people, Article II of the Constitution requires that the president and vice president be elected by winning the majority of votes in an Electoral College.[21]

The Electoral College consists of 538 electors: one for each of the 435 members of the House of Representatives and 100 senators, and three for the District of Columbia. When a candidate wins the most popular votes in a state, that candidate wins the states' electoral votes as well. The presidential candidate with at least an absolute majority (one over half the total) wins.[22]

George W. Bush knew how important voting numbers were, both the popular vote count and the electoral count. He had years of experience running his

SOURCE DOCUMENT

Section 1 (3). [The electors shall meet in their respective states, and vote by ballot for two persons, of whom one at least shall not be an inhabitant of the same state with them-selves. And they shall make a list of all the persons voted for, and of the number of votes for each; which list they shall sign and certify, and transmit sealed to the seat of the government of the United States, directed to the president of the Senate. The president of the Senate shall, in the pres-ence of the Senate and House of Representatives, open all the certificates, and the votes shall then be counted. The person having the greatest number of votes shall be the President, if such number be a majority of the whole num-ber of electors appointed; and if there be more than one who have such majority, and have an equal number of votes, then the House of Representatives shall immediately choose by ballot one of them for President; and if no per-son have a majority, then from the five highest on the list the said House shall in like manner choose the President. But in choosing the President, the votes shall be taken by states, the representation from each state having one vote; a quorum for this purpose shall consist of a member or members from two-thirds of the states, and a majority of all the states shall be necessary to a choice. In every case, after the choice of the President, the person having the greatest number of votes of the electors shall be the Vice President. But if there should remain two or more who have equal votes, the Senate shall choose from them by ballot the Vice President.]

Article II, Section 1 (3) of the United States Constitution explains the Electoral College.

own campaigns and running those of his father and of his father's friends.

To be president, Bush needed to win the popular vote in the key states with the highest number of electoral votes. George W. figured he was good for 300 to 310 electoral votes—and 270 were enough to win.[23]

During the 2000 campaign, Bush's key states included Ohio with 21 electoral votes, Pennsylvania with 23, Michigan with 18, Wisconsin and Washington each with 11, and Florida with 25. In more common terms, these states were "up for grabs." They did not consistently vote for one party. During the last ten presidential elections, each of these states, except Florida, had voted five times for a Republican nominee and five times for a Democratic one.

Of the key states, Florida offered the most electoral votes, 25. Weeks before election day, George W. Bush calculated how important winning Florida would be to his success. In the past ten elections, Florida voted Republican seven times.

George W. remained confident throughout the Florida ballot recount ordeal. His brother, Jeb Bush, was the governor of Florida. Jeb Bush had a "proven campaign apparatus ready to try to deliver the state" for his big brother George.[24]

The Florida recount process exploded into an "all-out war." It was a "whirlwind of more than fifty lawsuits, and appeals to every possible court, news conferences, protests, speeches, public hearings, private strategies and televised ballot-counting sessions."[25]

Some people questioned how much Jeb Bush helped his brother win Florida. They questioned Katherine Harris, Florida's secretary of state who was a registered Republican and served as co-chair of George W. Bush's campaign. As secretary of state, she was ultimately responsible for regulating and certifying the state's presidential election.[26]

Arguments flared. There were hot disagreements about how ballots in some Florida counties had been counted. Some critics said that the ballot's "butterfly" design confused many voters. A butterfly design squeezes many candidates' names onto an open two-page spread of a punch-card ballot. In Florida, six candidates were listed on the left side, and five candidates, including a write-in candidate spot, were listed on the right. The confusion was in the center between the two sides where ten punch holes ran. Alternately, numbered arrows pointed from left page names and right page names to their center punch holes. Many voters said that they might have accidentally voted for the wrong person.

Problems were reported in voting areas that used machines instead of punch cards. Some people said that voting machines were working improperly, especially in the predominately African-American counties in Florida. These counties were major supporters for Gore.[27]

"Chads" became a major focus. A chad is a perforated area, usually rectangular, next to a candidate's name in a punched ballot, which the voter punches to record a vote. The punch should knock the chad completely out of the ballot, leaving a hole. An election machine counts the number of holes. "Spoiled ballots" are ballots that the tabulating machinery does not record as votes, whether because of voter error, machine defects, or other factors.

Spoiled ballots include those with a hanging chad that is attached by only one corner; a swinging or dangling chad that hangs by two corners; a tri-chad that is attached by three corners; and a dimpled or pregnant chad, which while bulging, indented, or marked, remains attached to the ballot by all four corners.

In Florida, when the same ballots were hand-counted, debates arose on whether or not the human counters, who could see the chads, should count them as votes.

Another Florida issue was absentee ballots. For those who could not be at the voting booths, they requested a mail-in ballot. There was a mailing deadline. Any ballots mailed after that date would not be counted. Critics said absentee ballots were accepted and counted too late after election day. Others said that some people mailed their absentee ballots in and showed up at the polling booths and voted again.[28]

The debates were not to be decided by the state of Florida. The presidential outcome eventually rested with the U.S. Supreme Court. On December 11, 2000, a bitterly divided U.S. Supreme Court, in a 5–4 vote, effectively decided that George W. Bush had won the election. He would indeed become the forty-third president of the United States.

Two days later, President-elect George W. Bush began the process of bringing a divided nation together. He addressed the people. He knew that some people believed he had illegally taken the presidency from Al Gore.

To everyone, he said, "Vice President Gore and I put our hearts and hopes into our campaigns . . . so I understand how difficult this moment must be for Vice President Gore and his family." Bush spoke for unity. "Our votes may differ, but not our hopes. . . . We can unite and inspire the American citizens."[29]

January 20, 2001, was cold and wet. At the Capitol in Washington, D.C., George W. Bush was surrounded by people who supported him and those who did not. He spoke to everyone of the need to join together to face the challenges ahead. Pledging to uphold the ideals of the United States Constitution and its people, George W. Bush became the nation's forty-third president.

6

SETTING UP
HOUSE: THE
FIRST EIGHT
MONTHS

President George W. Bush's first weeks in office focused on establishing his personal style of leadership and completing the selection of his cabinet. In addition, he began to address issues on the economy, energy, and science.

President Bush spoke of his continuing effort to unify the country. "My job is to remind people that I'm going to be everybody's president." He said, "One of the things that people will learn about me is, I'm the kind of person that likes to get things done."[1]

George W. agreed that he had changed since he worked as a senior adviser to his father's presidential campaign in 1992. "I know what I want to do. And I'm

SOURCE DOCUMENT

President Clinton, distinguished guests and my fellow citizens, the peaceful transfer of authority is rare in history, yet common in our country. With a simple oath, we affirm old traditions and make new beginnings.

As I begin, I thank President Clinton for his service to our nation.

And I thank Vice President Gore for a contest conducted with spirit and ended with grace.

I am honored and humbled to stand here, where so many of America's leaders have come before me, and so many will follow.

We have a place, all of us, in a long story—a story we continue, but whose end we will not see. It is the story of a new world that became a friend and liberator of the old, a story of a slave-holding society that became a servant of freedom, the story of a power that went into the world to protect but not possess, to defend but not to conquer.

It is the American story—a story of flawed and fallible people, united across the generations by grand and enduring ideals.

On January 20, 2001, President George W. Bush gave his inaugural address. This is an excerpt from the beginning of his speech.

at peace because I've surrounded myself with a really magnificent group of people."[2]

Many of those "magnificent people" were members of his White House staff or Cabinet. Not only did they come as personal colleagues and friends of George W., some of them had also served as members of the staff of past presidents, including Gerald Ford, Ronald Reagan, and George H. W. Bush.

George W.'s Cabinet included Vice President Dick Cheney, who had spent ten years in the White House and served as George H. W. Bush's defense secretary. Karen Hughes worked with George W. ever since he ran for governor of Texas. Her job as counselor to the President was to oversee the president's schedule, the speech-writing corps, and press office. Longtime friend to the president, Karl Rove was senior adviser to the president. He helped George W. plot the course of his presidency.

Condoleezza Rice was assistant to the president for National Security Affairs. She was the first woman to head the National Security Council and was a key voice in advising Bush on when, and how, to intervene in trouble spots around the world. Ari Fleischer served as White House press secretary, and Andrew H. Card, as White House chief of staff.

Donald H. Rumsfeld was secretary of defense. Colin Powell, secretary of state, was one of the most admired men in the country. He served as the president's leading foreign-policy voice, but also planned to influence the revamping of the military and building of a missile defense system, as well as influence the president's decisions regarding other social and political issues.[3]

Other key advisers to the president included John D. Ashcroft, attorney general of the United States; General Tommy Franks, commander of U.S. forces' Central Command; George J. Tenet, director of the

George W. Bush appointed many women to positions of power. The first woman to head the National Security Council is Condoleezza Rice (left).

Central Intelligence Agency (CIA); and Robert S. Mueller III, director of the Federal Bureau of Investigation (FBI).

Additional staff positions included Ann Veneman, secretary of agriculture; Christie Todd Whitman, head of the Environmental Protection Agency; Paul O'Neill, secretary of the treasury; and Rod Paige, secretary of education.

President George W. Bush had appointed more women to positions of power than any president in history. His friends joked that Bush wound up surrounding himself with tough, straight-talking women who were a lot like his mother, Barbara Bush. President Bush said, "Part of the reason why I feel I value the advice of very strong-willed and strong-minded women is because of my mom."[4]

With the aid of his advisers, President Bush began to act on some of the issues that faced the United States. One of the issues dealt with the nation's economy. During his presidential campaign, George W. offered a tax cut program in an effort to give money back to taxpayers. The United States budget had a surplus of money, and Bush felt some of that surplus should go back into the pockets of Americans.

The people who criticized the idea said it was too grand of a plan. But, after several years of prosperity, a slowing economy began to take over the country. When Bush took office, economy experts said the slowdown, or recession, was nothing more than a temporary inconvenience. As the year continued, the economy worsened. President Bush's tax cut idea grew in popularity.[5]

President Bush predicted that tax cut money would encourage American consumers to spend more thereby helping the economy improve. Opponents argued that the wealthiest families would receive the best deal. Under Bush's plan, critics said, a low-income family would only receive about $200 and a middle-income family around $1,600. On the other hand, wealthier families would receive between $6,000 and $46,000 in tax cuts.[6] Other critics feared using up the budget surplus. Bush's plan would cost over $1.3 trillion. That price plus other programs and a falling economy could eat up the budget.[7]

Americans favored the tax cut, and throughout the summer 2001, Congress and the president worked out a tax cut plan.

Besides a falling economy, the nation had been experiencing a rise in energy prices. Many Americans saw their heating bills skyrocket. California endured massive rolling blackouts. Rather than asking Americans to turn down their thermostats or car manufacturers to create more fuel-efficient automobiles, President Bush's response was to boost energy production.[8]

He vowed to increase oil, gas, and coal production on federal lands and speed up the approval process for oil and gas production. Bush's aim was to receive Congressional approval to build a gas pipeline through Alaska's Arctic National Wildlife Refuge (ANWR). A 1998 geological survey estimated between 3 and 16 billion barrels of oil in the Alaskan refuge.[9]

The wildlife refuge was established in 1960 by President Dwight D. Eisenhower. It was seen as America's last unspoiled frontier. The area contains large populations of caribou, moose, musk oxen, wolves, fox, grizzly and polar bears, along with loons, snow geese, and many other species of migratory birds. In 1980, President Jimmy Carter doubled the refuge's size to 19 million acres.[10]

Bush's proposal angered many environment-friendly

Americans. They spoke of the animals whose lives depended on migrating through the very area where a pipeline was planned. Critics argued that it would take between ten to fifteen years before oil could be drilled and transported from Alaska to the rest of the United States. And then the amount of oil would only satisfy about 5 percent of Americans' daily oil usage.[11]

Some saw Bush as the most anti-environmental president since Ronald Reagan. George W. supported other anti-environment actions such as the dredging for gravel in protected wetlands and the continued use of snowmobiles in Yellowstone National Park.[12] He also withdrew the country from talks on a global-warming treaty called the Kyoto Protocol—an international agreement to cut emissions of carbon dioxide and other global-warming gases.

Another issue that faced the new President dealt with stem cell research. The issue was of serious concern to the scientific community and to the conservative religious groups.

Stem cells, which are no bigger than the dot on an *i* are taken from microscopic days-old embryos. The embryos are destroyed in the extraction process. Scientists envisioned using stem cells to grow a variety of tissues; for example, neurons to treat Alzheimer's disease, cardiac cells to replace tissue damaged by a heart attack, or insulin-producing pancreas cells to replace nonfunctioning cells in people who have diabetes.[13]

The religious right considered the destruction of the

embryos in the stem cell extraction process a destruction of human life. They believed the government should not fund any type of stem cell research. At the time, stem cell funding was done through privately raised money only.[14]

President Bush decided to fund limited embryonic stem cell research, thus walking a fine line between scientists eager to move forward with the research and the religious conservatives who hoped to ban it altogether.[15]

By May 1, 2001, George W. Bush had been president of the United States for one hundred days. His general approval rating by the American public was at 60 percent. When asked how he would rate his job performance so far, he said, "Pretty darn good."[16]

Other people agreed. On the tax issue, Bush was expected to receive from Congress at least 75 percent of what he wanted. He was also close to a deal on education reform that included putting billions of dollars into literacy programs.[17]

Considering the circumstances under which George W. Bush came into office, he had made respectable progress on his issues. Congress, evenly divided between Republicans and Democrats, also seemed to work with the president.

In early June 2001, President Bush began his first overseas tour. It was a five-day, five-country tour that included stops in Spain, Belgium, Sweden, Poland, and Slovenia.

Some people saw the trip as the White House's hope of bettering the president's image with allied nations. The pro-United States countries had become disappointed in some of Bush's decisions.[18]

Since coming into office, the president had broken off nonproliferation talks with North Korea. He was silent about South Korean president Kim Dae Jung's Nobel Peace Prize-winning efforts to reconcile with North Korea. And he abruptly announced the United States' withdrawal from the Kyoto Protocol on global warming.[19]

Of the five stops, President Bush especially looked forward to visiting King Juan Carlos, a friend of Bush's father, and Queen Sophia of Spain. He was also fascinated with meeting Russian president Vladimir Putin in Slovenia.

One foreign leader, Mexican president Vicente Fox Quesada, enjoyed working with President Bush. No other Mexican president had ever had the same positive chemistry with a United States president that President Fox had with George W. Bush.[20]

In September 2001, President Vicente Fox prepared to be President Bush's first state visitor. Their agenda was to discuss a new U.S. immigration policy for Mexico.[21]

However, their meeting would not occur as planned, nor would any regular business take place in the White House or on Capitol Hill. The whole country would seem to stop for one nightmarish day when the greatest challenge of George W. Bush's presidency, as well as his life, hit on September 11, 2001.

7

A TEST OF STRENGTH AND ABILITY

George W. Bush fought hard to win the presidential election. In his eight months as president, he believed he was doing a pretty good job. But his leadership abilities and his personal strength were truly tested as he began to take action against the terrorist attacks of September 11, 2001.

President Bush had to accomplish many tasks at once. He had to find out who was behind the four hijacked plane attacks. He had to make sure that no additional attacks occurred. He also had to reassure a nation of emotionally upset people that their president was able to handle the crisis.

To assist him, President Bush created special committees. The committees worked with many U.S. government officials, military departments, and foreign communications groups. Thousands of trained people were called into action. Bush's committees coordinated their efforts. The committees reported to the president.

One committee included mainly military generals. They were familiar with terrorist attack groups. Led by General Richard Myers, chairman of the Joint Chiefs of Staff, the committee helped develop America's military response to the attackers of September 11.

Another committee dealt with the exchange of information between the United States and foreign countries. The members understood propaganda. They worked to decide what messages contained truthful information and what messages did not. They made arrangements for U.S. officials to speak on foreign television shows. The committee was called the CIC, or the Coalition Information Center.

President Bush appointed Pennsylvania's governor Tom Ridge to head another committee. Bush called this group Homeland Security. Tom Ridge coordinated investigations into security measures within the United States. He suggested ways to make America safe from future attacks. His committee also aided the search to find other possible terrorists who could still be in the United States.

President Bush knew that he needed a lot of money to fund the work of these committees. He also wanted stricter law enforcement measures and tighter airline security procedures. Bush went to Congress and asked

SOURCE DOCUMENT

Executive Order
Establishing the Office of Homeland Security and the Homeland Security Council

By the authority vested in me as President by the Constitution and the laws of the United States of America, it is hereby ordered as follows:

Section 1. Establishment. I hereby establish within the Executive Office of the President an Office of Homeland Security (the "Office") to be headed by the Assistant to the President for Homeland Security.

Sec. 2. Mission. The mission of the Office shall be to develop and coordinate the implementation of a comprehensive national strategy to secure the United States from terrorist threats or attacks. The Office shall perform the functions necessary to carry out this mission, including the functions specified in section 3 of this order.

Sec. 3. Functions. The functions of the Office shall be to coordinate the executive branch's efforts to detect, prepare for, prevent, protect against, respond to, and recover from terrorist attacks within the United States.

After the attacks of September 11, 2001, George W. Bush created many new committees and groups. This executive order established the Office of Homeland Security.

for $20 billion. Bush said he would do "whatever it takes" to get the terrorists and to preserve America.[1]

By the morning of September 12, 2001, the CIA and the FBI had evidence of connections between at least three of the nineteen hijackers and Osama bin Laden and his training camps in Afghanistan. It was consistent with intelligence reporting all summer showing that bin Laden had been planning "spectacular attacks" against U.S. targets.[2]

Osama bin Laden grew up in Saudi Arabia, the son of a very wealthy construction designer. When Osama bin Laden was a young adult, his father died, leaving bin Laden a multimillionaire. As he got older, he became a strong believer of the radical fundamentalism of the religion.[3]

His version of modern Islam included spreading fundamentalism throughout the Middle East, raging against the spoiling of Islamic soil by unbelievers, and leading a "jihad," or holy war, through terrorism against any unbelievers outside the Islamic world.[4]

Osama bin Laden left Saudi Arabia for Afghanistan in 1979 to help defend Afghanistan from invasion by the Soviet Union. He created al Qaeda, which is Arabic for "the base." It began as a fund-raising organization for terrorist groups.[5]

By 1996, Osama bin Laden's al Qaeda had joined forces with the ruling party of Afghanistan, the Taliban. They began building a network of terrorist training camps throughout the country.[6]

President Bush demanded that Afghanistan's Taliban surrender bin Laden and let the United States into the terrorists' camps. In Afghanistan and throughout the world, Bush threatened to stop anyone connected with al Qaeda. In a speech to Congress and to the American people, George W. Bush said, "These demands are not open to negotiations or discussion. The Taliban must act, and act immediately. They will hand over the terrorists, or they will share in their fate."[7]

George W. Bush also planned to send American troops to Afghanistan to capture or destroy Osama bin Laden and his terrorist armies. He said that a U.S. military strike would come soon. "Be ready," he told the military.

While deciding how to best handle Osama bin Laden and his terrorist forces, Bush knew he had to ease the minds of Americans. He had to reassure them that he understood what they were experiencing.

President Bush declared Friday, September 14, 2001, a national day of mourning and remembrance. Dignitaries gathered at the National Cathedral in Washington, D.C., for a morning service. Past presidents Bill Clinton, George H. W. Bush, Jimmy Carter, and Gerald Ford attended. Religious evangelist and Bush family friend, the Reverend Billy Graham, gave the sermon.

In a speech to the gathering and to the world, President George W. Bush promised everyone, "Our responsibility to history is already clear: to answer these attacks and rid the world of evil."[8]

After the service, Bush flew to New York City.

Under tight security, an enormous motorcade of fifty-five vehicles drove the president past cheering and flag-waving crowds to the sixteen-acre site of destruction called Ground Zero. Under his feet, more than 2,800 people still lay buried, along with 343 firefighters, and 91 fire trucks.[9]

The president hugged rescue workers, shook hands,

SOURCE DOCUMENT

We are here in the middle hour of our grief. So many have suffered so great a loss, and today we express our nation's sorrow. We come before God to pray for the missing and the dead, and for those who love them.

On Tuesday, our country was attacked with deliberate and massive cruelty. We have seen the images of fire and ashes, and bent steel.

Now come the names, the list of casualties we are only beginning to read. They are the names of men and women who began their day at a desk or in an airport, busy with life. They are the names of people who faced death, and in their last moments called home to say, be brave, and I love you.

They are the names of passengers who defied their murderers, and prevented the murder of others on the ground. They are the names of men and women who wore the uniform of the United States, and died at their posts.

Shown here is an excerpt of President Bush's remarks on September 14, 2001.

and spoke encouraging words to all. Although he had talked to many others about the devastation, he still was not prepared for what he found. It was "a nightmare, a living nightmare," the president said.[10]

He had not planned to speak to the crowd, and there was no microphone. But he was drawn to say something. Someone handed him a white bullhorn, and he stood on top of a burnt fire truck. While he spoke, voices kept yelling that they could not hear him. Nevertheless, President Bush said, "I can hear you. The rest of the world hears you, and the people who knocked these buildings down will hear all of us soon."[11]

That evening at Camp David, President Bush met with his most senior national security advisers: Dick Cheney, Colin Powell, Donald Rumsfeld, and Condoleezza Rice. Together they prepared for the weekend's meeting with the president's Cabinet to plan a war strategy in Afghanistan.

The planning, discussion, and outcome would become a defining moment of George W. Bush's presidency, and he knew it.

He told his advisers of his decisions:

> This is the primary focus of this administration . . . it doesn't matter to me how long it takes, we're going to route out terror wherever it may exist . . . the doctrine is, if you harbor them, feed them, house them, you're just as guilty, and you will be held to account . . . this war will be fought on many fronts, including the intelligence side, the financial side, the diplomatic side, as well as the military side . . . we're going to hit them with all we've got in a smart way.[12]

President Bush shakes hands, thanking those who helped in the rescue effort at Ground Zero.

On October 7, 2001, Bush ordered the first air and ground troops to attack Afghanistan. The United States military campaign had officially begun. The troops found it difficult to maneuver in the country's terrain. The ruling Taliban and al Qaeda armies were sometimes impossible to get to. George W. Bush knew that the American attack against Osama bin Laden and his followers was going to last longer than he had hoped.

In order to wage a war on terrorism abroad and deal with terrorism at home, President Bush supported widening the powers of his federal workers. He and his Cabinet drew up a plan and presented it to Congress for approval. The issue involved restricting the civil liberties or freedoms of the people in America for the sake of national security.

Attorney General Ashcroft answered many questions from Congress as he testified in favor of the president's plan. Changes were made to the final bill.

On October 25, 2001, Senate approved, 98–1, the USA Patriot Act that gave Attorney General Ashcroft much of what he had asked for, including provisions that:

1) Allow "roving wiretaps" that follow suspects no matter what telephone they use. The old rule required a new warrant for each phone. The provision "sunsets," or ends in 2005;

2) Give law enforcement the authority to conduct "secret searches" of a suspect's residence, including computer files. Authorities can delay telling the suspect of the source for "a reasonable time" if such information would adversely affect the investigation. Previously, law enforcement had to inform suspects of any search;

3) Allow the attorney general to detain any non-citizen believed to be a national security risk for up to seven days without being charged for something. After seven days the government must charge the suspect or begin deportation proceedings. If the suspect cannot be deported, the government can continue the detention so long as the attorney general certifies that the suspect is a national security risk every six months;

4) Make it illegal for someone to harbor an individual they know or should have known had engaged in or was about to engage in a terrorist act;

5) Give the Treasury Department new powers and banks and depositors new responsibilities in tracking the movement of money;

6) Allow investigators to share secret grand jury information or information obtained through wire-taps with government officials if it is important for counterintelligence or foreign intelligence operations; and

7) Allow authorities to track Internet communications (e-mail) as they do telephone calls.[13]

The USA Patriot Act caused disagreement with people and organizations that feared that the federal government would abuse the rules. Critics pointed out that within a few weeks of the September 11 attacks, the Justice Department had detained over twelve hundred immigrants, mainly Muslim, and had about half of them still in detention weeks later with no formal charge.[14]

Another issue that caused controversy was President Bush's desire to use military tribunals to try those people suspected of terrorist acts. Military tribunals have been used in past military conflicts and were generally conducted in secret, using military personnel rather than civilians for its judges and juries.

Critics disapproved of military tribunals. They claimed that such tribunals were unconstitutional and unfair for several reasons. The trials would be held in secret. The evidence and the proof would not have to be very convincing. Only two thirds of a jury would be needed to approve an execution, not a unanimous vote as needed in regular American trials.

Supporters for military tribunals pointed out that given the threat that al Qaeda posed to the general population, it would not be wise to subject judicial personnel and citizen jurors to the potentially lifelong consequences of involvement in a war crimes trial when military tribunals were an accepted alternative.[15]

Polls showed that American people generally supported the steps taken by President Bush's administration since September 11. They also tended to believe that in times of war the restriction of certain liberties was to be expected.[16]

By December 7, 2001, the last of the known Taliban strongholds in Afghanistan fell. The United States and its allied forces were basically in charge of the country. The event made front-page news; however, the President had promised no celebration, no parades, no surrender signing ceremony.[17]

Although the U.S. government began actions to install a new governing power in Afghanistan, there was still a ways to go before President Bush could declare a victory in the war on terrorism. At the end of 2001, sixteen of the twenty-two top leaders of al Qaeda were still not captured, including Osama bin Laden.[18]

8

DEALING WITH DOMESTIC ISSUES

As President George W. Bush engaged the country in a military retaliation against the foreign attacks of September 11 on American soil, in October 2001, he faced another attack within the country itself. The threat was anthrax poisoning, which was a disease long associated with biological warfare.

For four days, a man in Florida struggled against inhalation anthrax until he died on October 5, 2001. His coworker was also infected.[1] The FBI was called in for a full investigation. Anthrax began making front-page news.

A week later, an assistant to Tom Brokaw, anchorman for NBC, contracted anthrax from a letter. On the same day, a letter opened in the Capitol Building in the offices of Senate majority leader Tom Daschle tested positive for traces of anthrax.

Someone or some group within the United States was mailing envelopes containing a deadly white powder that, once inhaled, could very easily cause death.

Meanwhile, a Washington, D.C., mail clerk had handled an envelope containing anthrax and fell ill. He went to the hospital that night. The doctors believed he had the flu and sent him home with medicine. He died the next day.

By the week's end, thirty-five postal facilities had to be tested. Police announced that anthrax was found in three more offices in Congress. House Speaker Dennis Hastert ordered the Capitol Building closed. Special crews were called in to test for anthrax and to disinfect every room in the building.

A month later, according to a report from the Center for Disease Control and Prevention, sixteen people were infected with anthrax and another four had died.[2] People were given antibiotics, yet health officials did not have a cure.

President Bush's new committee, Homeland Security, was given the job of coordinating the investigation of the anthrax threats. Homeland Security's task forces struggled to find answers. Law enforcement agencies responded to an estimated ten thousand chemical and biological hoaxes in October 2001 alone after the first man in Florida died from anthrax on October 5.[3]

The anthrax killings persuaded the Food and Drug Administration (FDA) to approve an anthrax vaccine

GOVERNOR RIDGE: Good afternoon. I want to update you on the anthrax situation here in the District of Columbia and then brief you on specific steps we are taking around the country to protect our postal workers and our citizens. The residents of Washington, D.C., and all Americans can be confident that their government is taking every step possible to ensure that our mail systems are safe and that they are secure.

A short while ago, I briefed the President with the latest facts on the anthrax situation, as we know them. Here are those facts. First, two postal employees who work at the Brentwood mail facility here in Washington, D.C., have tested positive for inhalation anthrax. Both of these workers are being treated with antibiotics, and obviously our best wishes and prayers are with them and their families.

In October 2001, the director of Homeland Security, Tom Ridge, discussed the anthrax threats and what was being done about the situation.

facility and prompted the federal government to increase its spending on biodefense by $6 billion.[4] The money gave researchers the opportunity to speed their progress toward discovering new vaccines and therapies as well as increase their understanding of how the anthrax bacterium grows.[5]

Unfortunately, the anthrax scare also pulled needed law enforcement people away from other areas of the country, and it also created panic in the United States Postal Service.[6]

The anthrax dilemma and the terrorist attacks of September 11 seemed to widen another increasing problem for President Bush. That problem was the economy.

Bush's early tax cut plan that put money in most Americans' pockets had not stimulated the economy as hoped. Instead of improving, the economy worsened. Employers cut 468,000 jobs in October 2001, then 331,000 in November. By January 2002, the end of his first year in office, President Bush saw the U.S. unemployment rate jump to 5.7 percent. It was the highest rate in six years.[7]

President Bush blamed the economic slump on the Democrats for their expensive government programs. The Democrats blamed the president for his expensive tax cut.

The poor economy and the military conflict in Afghanistan also contributed to a rise in gasoline prices. Americans in some places were paying over two dollars a gallon for gas. The situation helped President Bush's support for oil drilling in the Arctic National Wildlife Refuge. The push reheated political, economic, and environmental debates on the issue.

But there was more than the economy and Afghanistan to be concerned about. What increased the worries of the American people was the threat of a new war.

9

WAR ON IRAQ AND ON TERRORISM

A merican citizens began to hear of a threat of a new war on January 29, 2002, during President Bush's first State of the Union address. He said that he aimed to prevent governments that sponsored terror from threatening the United States, its friends, and allies through the use of weapons of mass destruction.

President Bush specified three countries: North Korea, Iran, and Iraq. He said that their regimes made up an "axis of evil."[1]

The president's comments received strong reactions. The Middle Eastern country of Jordan supported Bush's goal. Other countries insisted on seeing the evidence that the three countries possessed weapons of mass destruction and planned on using them. North Korea stated that the president's words were "little short of a declaration of war."[2]

President Bush spoke more words in his speech against Iraq. Iraq's leader Saddam Hussein had been a target of U.S. hostility for over ten years, going back to when George H. W. Bush was president.

In 1990, Iraq invaded Kuwait. President George H. W. Bush intervened using United States military force in a conflict called the Gulf War. Although the war never killed Saddam Hussein, his invasion was stopped and his growing power was restricted.

A cease-fire demanded that Iraq destroy all chemical, biological, and nuclear weapons. Furthermore, an inspection team from the United Nations would make periodic checks on Saddam Hussein to insure his compliance.

George H. W. Bush, seen here with General Norman Schwarzkopf, intervened with military force in 1990 when Iraq invaded Kuwait.

Iraq did not go along with the cease-fire. As a result, the United Nations put sanctions on the country's government. Iraq, the second richest country in known oil reserves in the world, could not trade its oil for anything but food, medical supplies, and basic necessities for its civilians.[3]

After twelve years, anger against Saddam Hussein's regime was renewed. By summer 2002, President Bush's threat to initiate a war with Iraq grew more urgent.

In response to President Bush, the United Nations sent its inspection team to find evidence that Iraq was once again making weapons of mass destruction. The team's report found no conclusive evidence that Saddam Hussein was building such an arsenal.[4]

Supporters and opponents spoke out strongly as the possibility of a war grew more real.

Supporters for Bush's position believed that Iraq would continue to defy any spoken or written resolutions against it. Saddam Hussein already had defied sixteen other resolutions made by the United Nations since 1990. Supporters also believed that it would be best to stop Iraq before it attacked the United States or another country. Furthermore, under such a tyrant, the people of Iraq would be free only through war. And the only way to stop Saddam Hussein was through war.[5]

Opponents did not believe Iraq had weapons of mass destruction. They also felt that a war with Iraq would lead to many American casualties and would not end quickly.[6] Furthermore, the United States was still fighting terrorism in Afghanistan, and another military conflict could endanger the progress the U.S. had made in taking out al Qaeda.[7]

Some analysts questioned why President Bush was driven to oust Saddam Hussein when there was clear evidence that another "axis of evil" country, North Korea had weapons of mass destruction.

North Korea's dictator Kim Jong Il was ruthless and controlled large stocks of chemical and biological weapons and some crude nuclear devices. He threatened to use them against the United States or to sell them to other terrorists.[8]

President Bush did not see Kim Jong Il as great as a concern as Saddam Hussein in Iraq. He said that the dictator's threat was false. If anything, he was blackmailing the United States, said the president.[9]

In mid-October 2002, Congress approved language that granted President George W. Bush the power to act militarily. Before the president could give the command to war, he had to certify that all diplomatic or other peaceful means to protect against the Iraqi threat had been exhausted.[10]

In his State of the Union address in January 2003, the president reinforced the need to stop Saddam Hussein before he attacked. Bush described some of the evidence proving Iraq to possess advanced weapons programs. The written proof came from intelligence sources in the United States and other countries.[11]

On March 20, 2003, U.S. military forces began bombing Baghdad, Iraq. Quickly, much of the city was destroyed. Saddam Hussein was gone, but no evidence confirmed his death.

The regime of Saddam Hussein did not last long under U.S. military actions. The aftermath, however, was a long, seemingly unending struggle. After buildings were hit by U.S. bombs, looters came in and stole property from hospitals and destroyed museums and other offices and buildings. Electricity and telephones rarely worked. The water was unhealthy. People had trouble getting gasoline for their cars.

In May 2003, President Bush declared that combat operations in Iraq were over. The United States and a coalition of allied nations were engaged in securing and reconstructing the country. George W. Bush announced an interim director to take over operating Iraq.[12]

The toppling of Saddam Hussein did not stop the fighting. American soldiers continued to be attacked and killed by Iraqi people. There was dangerous unrest throughout the country. President Bush's war commander, General Tommy Franks, suggested that the United States would need to remain in Iraq for perhaps four years in an effort to restore order in the country.[13]

Months after the United States entered Iraq, American military experts still had not produced evidence that Iraq had weapons of mass destruction.[14]

Critics questioned the legitimacy of foreign intelligence sources that gave documentation of Iraq possessing the materials to build nuclear weapons. U.S. officials said the documentation was forged.[15]

President George W. Bush remained confident in his leadership role. He believed in his decision to attack Iraq. He said, "History and time will prove that the United States made the absolute right decision in freeing the people of Iraq from the clutches of Saddam Hussein."[16]

While the president dealt with the situation in Iraq, the country's war on terrorism in Afghanistan had not ceased since it began in October 2001.

Some critics called the U.S. mission in Afghanistan a failure. They noted the growth of warlords, criminal Islamists, illegal-drug trafficking, and general lawlessness

George W. Bush shakes hands with soldiers, thanking them.

that had spread over the Middle Eastern country. On the other hand, other critics, who agreed that intense challenges still existed, pointed out the progress that America's military had made so far.[17]

The foremost objective to oust the Taliban and al Qaeda was successful. Military forces had killed or captured around 2,000 of the 10,000 terrorist soldiers who were inside Afghanistan at the time of the initial U.S. attack.[18] The American forces destroyed the Taliban government and drove al Qaeda into the frontier areas of Pakistan.[19]

The United States, along with help from the United Nations and other nongovernmental organizations, stemmed a mass famine that had been predicted to occur in the fall of 2001. The U.S. also distributed tons of hybrid seeds throughout Afghanistan, even to the country's most remote parts. The seeds provided a new beginning to the country's agriculture.[20]

Although thousands of acres of land were still full of land mines, America's military forces destroyed ten thousand mines in Kandahar province alone and continued to work on the removal of more.[21]

To stop the growing warlord gangs and to ensure security, the American forces continued to train a professional army and institute a large program for police training. In addition, the U.S. provided money and help in reconstructing major highways and assisted in setting up a money system, education system, airline system, and legal-trade system throughout Afghanistan. The

U.S. believed that over time strong legal systems would overtake the lawlessness ones.[22]

Because of the improvements to the country, more than 2 million Afghan refugees willingly returned to their homes from refugee camps in Pakistan and Iran.[23]

Some of the commanders of the American troops were not optimistic when they thought of what would happen to the country when the United States pulled out of Afghanistan. Some believed the terrorist-soldier training camps could easily be set up again once the U.S. was gone.[24]

Many difficult problems and dangerous situations still existed in Afghanistan. However, President Bush believed that his efforts to lead the United States into a military attack on terrorism and especially an attack on the Taliban government were successful.

10

THE RIGHT MAN
FOR THE JOB

After a controversial election, forty-third president George W. Bush stood tall and helped the United States through difficult times. September 11, 2001, will be a date for all to remember, and the actions resulting from those terrorist attacks will help define Bush's legacy. In addition, Bush has had to deal with image problems and complex domestic problems.

In March 2003, Bush made his newly formed Department of Homeland Security an official government office.

The new department's purpose is complex. One of its main responsibilities is to prevent future terrorist strikes. That requires dealing with all the airline travelers, cargo containers, and border crossers across the nation. The department is also assigned the task of helping with natural disasters such as hurricanes and tornadoes.

President Bush said to Homeland Security Director Tom Ridge and his employees, "You've accepted a difficult mission. But I'm confident of the success of our efforts because I'm confident in you."[1]

By spring 2003, the public's confidence in the economy dropped to a nine-year low. Added to the worries, was the nation's budget problems. The surplus of money that had encouraged Bush's tax cut program in the summer of 2001 was now gone. What was left of the country's savings was earmarked for Social Security and Medicare payments for America's aged, retired, and otherwise qualified citizens. The public feared the loss of these benefits if the government needed to support its other programs.[2]

George W. Bush has led the nation through good times and bad times.

Handling the country's domestic and foreign problems such as the economy and terrorism, George W. Bush took his responsibilities as commander in chief more seriously than anything else in his life. In his personal life, Bush tried to keep some of his daily routines. He read his Bible every morning for inspiration, took midday runs, lifted weights, ate as healthily as he could, and got plenty of sleep. He also made sure that he had time to relax at Camp David or at his ranch in Texas.[3]

But George W.'s laughter and joking did not come to him as quickly as it once did. Instead of reading books of personal interest, he took government briefing books and office memos to his room and read them before going to sleep each night.[4]

The challenges of running the country demanded his serious attention, but George W. believed that he was the right man for the job. He was confident that he made America a better and stronger country.[5]

CHRONOLOGY

1946—Born in New Haven, Connecticut, on July 6.

1948—Moves to Odessa, Texas.

1950—Moves to "Easter Egg Row" in Midland, Texas.

1953—Sister Robin dies of leukemia, at age 3.

1961—Attends Phillips Academy in Andover,
–1968 Massachusetts.

1964—Attends Yale University graduating with a major
–1973 in history.

1968—Accepted into the Texas Air National Guard;
–1975 becomes F-102 pilot.

1972—Works for Project PULL in Houston.

1973—Attends Harvard University, earning a master's
degree in business administration.

1977—Meets librarian Laura Welch and marries her
three months later, on November 5.

1978— First campaign for U.S. Congress; wins primary
but loses election; starts own oil business,
Arbusto.

1980—Father becomes vice president.

1981—Twins, Jenna and Barbara, are born on
November 25.

1984—Becomes general manager and 1.8 percent
owner of Texas Rangers.

1988—Political adviser for father's presidential campaign; father wins.

1992—Father runs for reelection but loses to Bill Clinton.

1994—Runs for governor of Texas and wins against Ann Richards.

1998—Runs for reelection and wins in a landslide.

2000—August: Nominated presidential candidate at Republican Convention in Philadelphia, Pennsylvania.

November 7, election day: results too close to call a winner.

December 11: U.S. Supreme Court decision makes George W. the president-elect.

2001—January 20, inauguration day: Bush sworn in as forty-third president.

September 11: Terrorists hijack four passenger planes and crash into the World Trade Center in New York City, the Pentagon in Virginia, and a field in Pennsylvania.

September 12: Asks Congress for $20 billion to "do what it takes" to clean up the destruction and go after those responsible for the hijackings.

September 14: Declares a national day of mourning and remembrance; visits the World Trade Center site.

October 7: Orders air and ground troops to attack Afghanistan; battles outbreak of anthrax poisoning.

2002—October: Congress gives president powers to act militarily against Iraq.

2003—March: Bombing begins in Iraq; Homeland Security made a federal department.

June: Experts unable to find evidence of weapons of mass destruction in Iraq.

DID YOU KNOW?

Trivia from the President's lifetime

Did you know the movie *It's a Wonderful Life* starring Jimmy Stewart was released in 1946?

Did you know rock and roll emerged as a music style in the 1950s?

Did you know the Berlin Wall separating non-Communist West Berlin from Communist East Berlin in Germany was built in 1961? In 1989, the Wall was torn down unifying the city.

Did you know home computers, then called microcomputers, became popular in the late 1970s?

Did you know Music Television (MTV) was launched in 1981?

Did you know the first mammal to be successfully cloned was a sheep in 1996?

CHAPTER NOTES

Chapter 1. "Today Our Nation Saw Evil"

1. *The New York Times, A Nation Challenged: A Visual History of 9/11 and its Aftermath* (New York: Callaway, 2002), pp. 46–47.

2. Bob Woodward, *Bush at War* (New York: Simon and Schuster, 2002), p. 16.

3. Ibid., pp. 24–25.

4. William Safire, "Inside the Bunker," *New York Times*, September 13, 2001, p. A27.

5. Jim Debrose, "I've Never Seen the President So Angry or So Determined," *Springfield News-Sun*, September 16, 2001, p. 13.

6. *The New York Times*, pp. 44, 47.

7. Woodward, pp. 26–27.

8. Ibid., p. 28.

9. Elisabeth Bumiller, "A Somber Bush Says Terrorism Cannot Prevail," *New York Times*, September 12, 2001, p. A1.

10. Steven Erlanger, "European Nations Stand With U.S., Ready to Respond," *New York Times*, September 12, 2001, p. A23.

Chapter 2. Growing Up in Texas and New England

1. Bill Minutaglio, *First Son: George W. Bush and the Bush Family Dynasty* (New York: Times Books, 1999), p. 24.

2. Ibid., p. 145.

3. Ibid., p. 23.

4. Elizabeth Mitchell, *W: Revenge of the Bush Dynasty* (New York: Hyperion, 2000), pp. 11–13.

5. Janet Cawley, "George W. Bush and Al Gore: Head to Head," *Biography Magazine*, October 2000, pp. 62–63.

6. Herbert S. Parmet, *George W. Bush: The Life of a Lone Star Yankee* (New York: Scribner, 1997), p. 47.

7. George [H. W.] Bush with Victor Gold, *Looking Forward* (New York: Doubleday, 1987), p. 39.

8. Minutaglio, p. 25.

9. Ibid., p. 28.

10. Daniel Cohen, *George W. Bush: The Family Business* (Brookfield, Conn.: The Millbrook Press, Inc., 2000), p. 10.

11. Minutaglio, p. 49.

12. Cohen, p. 8.

13. Minutaglio, p. 7.

14. Ibid., p. 147.

15. Ibid., p. 19.

16. Mitchell, p. 44.

17. Minutaglio, p. 37.

18. Ibid., p. 159.

19. Mitchell, p. 49.

20. Ibid., p. 53.

21. Ibid., p. 58.

22. Ibid., p. 50.

23. Minutaglio, p. 71.

24. Ibid., p. 86.

25. Ibid., p. 91.

26. Ibid., p. 95.

27. Minutaglio, p. 102.

28. Ibid., p. 116.

29. Ibid., p. 121.

30. Cohen, p. 14.

31. Mitchell, p. 120.

Chapter 3. Early Political Moves

1. Dotson Rader, "I'm Not Afraid to Seize the Moment," *Parade*, April 29, 2001, p. 4.

2. Elizabeth Mitchell, *W: Revenge of the Bush Dynasty* (New York: Hyperion, 2000), p. 138.

3. Ibid.

4. Bill Minutaglio, *First Son: George W. Bush and the Bush Family Dynasty* (New York: Times Books, 1999), p. 160.

5. Ibid., p. 163.

6. Janet Cawley, "George W. Bush and Al Gore: Head to Head," *Biography Magazine*, October 2000, p. 67.

7. Minutaglio, p. 164.

8. Ibid., pp. 199–200.

9. Ibid., pp. 169–170.

10. Ibid., p. 168.

11. Mitchell, p. 153.

12. Ibid., p. 161.

13. Minutaglio, p. 184.

14. Mitchell, p. 171.

15. Ibid., p. 169.

16. Ibid., p. 175.

17. Ibid., p. 183.

18. George W. Bush, *A Charge to Keep* (New York: William and Morrow and Co., 1999), p. 85.

19. Minutaglio, p. 210.

20. Daniel Cohen, *George W. Bush: The Family Business* (Brookfield, Conn.: The Millbrook Press, Inc., 2000), p. 27.

21. Minutaglio, p. 210.

22. Mitchell, p. 230.

23. Minutaglio, p. 214.

24. Ibid., p. 224.

25. Ibid., p. 223.

26. Mitchell, pp. 223–224.

27. Ibid., p. 219.

28. Cohen, p. 28.

29. Mitchell, p. 231.

30. Ibid., p. 234.

Chapter 4. From Baseball Manager to Texas Governor

1. Bill Minutaglio, *First Son: George W. Bush and the Bush Family Dynasty* (New York: Times Books, 1999), p. 240.

2. Elizabeth Mitchell, *W: Revenge of the Bush Dynasty* (New York: Hyperion, 2000), pp. 247–248.

3. Ibid., p. 236.

4. Minutaglio, p. 322.

5. Daniel Cohen, *George W. Bush: The Family Business* (Brookfield, Conn.: The Millbrook Press, Inc., 2000), p. 35.

6. Minutaglio, p. 8.

7. J. H. Hatfield, *Fortunate Son: George W. Bush and the Making of an American President* (New York: Soft Skull Press, 2001), p. 120.

8. Minutaglio, pp. 268–269.

9. Ibid., p. 268.

10. Minutaglio, p. 288.

11. Minutaglio, p. 279.

12. Michael Barone, Richard E. Cohen, et. al., *Almanac of American Politics: 2002* (Washington, D.C.: National Journal, 2001), p. 52.

13. Minutaglio, p. 293.

14. Ibid., p. 294.

15. Mitchell, p. 326.

16. Ibid., p. 320.

17. Hatfield, p. 204.

18. Mitchell, p. 320.

19. Hatfield, p. 196.

20. Mitchell, p. 320.

Chapter 5. A Presidential Contender

1. Elizabeth Mitchell, *Revenge of the Bush Dynasty* (New York: Hyperion, 2000), p. 331.

2. Bill Minutaglio, *First Son: George W. Bush and the Bush Family Dynasty* (New York: Times Books, 1999), p. 320.

3. Janet Cawley, "George W. Bush and Al Gore: Head to Head," *Biography Magazine*, October 2000, p. 120.

4. Minutaglio, p. 312.

5. J. H. Hatfield, *Fortunate Son: George W. Bush and the Making of an American President* (New York: Soft Skull Press, 2001), pp. 283–284.

6. Ibid., p. 293.

7. Ibid., p. 288.

8. Ibid., p. 291.

9. Paul Alexander, *Man of the People: The Life of John McCain* (Hoboken, New Jersey: John Wiley and Sons, Inc., 2003), p. 220.

10. Ibid., p. 265.

11. Ibid., p. 307.

12. Ibid., p. 317.

13. George W. Bush, *A Charge to Keep* (New York: William Morrow and Company, 1999), p. 236.

14. Michael Barone, Richard E. Cohen, et. al., *The Almanac of American Politics: 2002* (Washington, D.C.: National Journal, 2001), p. 50.

15. The Political Staff of *The Washington Post*, "Deadlock: The Inside Story of America's Closest Election" (New York: Public Affairs, 2001), p. 17.

16. Ibid., p. 10.

17. Ibid., p. 32.

18. Ibid., p. 19.

19. Ibid., p. vii.

20. Ibid., pp. 20–21.

21. Richard A. Posner, *Breaking the Deadlock* (Princeton, N.J.: Princeton University Press, 2001), pp. 31–32.

22. Joseph M. Bessette and R. Kent Rasmussen, eds. "Electoral College," *Encyclopedia of American Government.* Vol. II (Pasedena, Cal.: Salem Press, Inc., 1998), p. 243.

23. The Political Staff of *The Washington Post*, p. 26.

24. Ibid., p. 5.

25. Ibid., p. 21.

26. Merzer, Martin and the Staff of *The Miami Herald, The Miami Herald Report: Democracy Held Hostage* (New York: St. Martin's Press, 2001), p. 133.

27. Ibid., pp. 80, 87.

28. Ibid., pp. 97–98.

29. "Governor George W. Bush Delivers Remarks," CNN News Internet site, December 13, 2000, <http://www.cnn.com/ELECTION/2000/transcripts/121300/bush.html>, (June 28, 2002).

Chapter 6. Setting Up House: The First Eight Months

1. Martha Brant and T. Trent Gegax, "Bush: I'm Going to Be Everybody's President," *Newsweek*, January 22, 2001, p. 26.

2. Kenneth T. Walsh, "Bush Redux," *U.S. News and World Report*, January 22, 2001, p. 15.

3. Norman Jean Roy, "Team Bush," *Newsweek*, January 22, 2001, pp. 30–35.

4. Martha Brant, "Bush's 'Power Puff' Girls," *Newsweek*, May 7, 2001, p. 36.

5. Robert J. Samuelson, "Looming Storm?" *Newsweek*, January 22, 2001, p. 36.

6. "What's in It For You?" *Newsweek*, February 19, 2001, pp. 20–21.

7. Douglas Waller, John F. Dickerson, and Karen Tumulty, "What is That Oink, Oink?" *Time*, February 19, 2001, p. 31.

8. David Whitman, Marianne Lavelle, and Joshua Kurlantzick, "Pumped for More Drilling," *U.S. News and World Report*, February 12, 2001, p. 36.

9. Terry McCarthy, Ann Blackman, and John F. Dickerson, "War Over Arctic Oil," *Time*, February 19, 2001, p. 27.

10. Ibid.

11. Robert J. Samuelson, "Energy War Within Us," *Newsweek*, May 28, 2001, p. 29.

12. Howard Fineman, "W's Green War," *Newsweek*, April 23, 2001, pp. 26–27.

13. "Stem Cell Research: Confronting Scientific and Moral Issues," Foreword, *Congressional Digest*, October 2001, p. 225.

14. Howard Fineman, Debra Rosenberg, and Martha Brant, "Bush Draws a Stem Cell Line," *Newsweek*, August 20, 2001, p. 17.

15. "Stem Cell Research," p. 225.

16. Evan Thomas, "First Brush With History," *Newsweek*, May 7, 2001, p. 29.

17. Lee Walczak and Richard S. Dunham, "Bush's Accidental, Unprepared, Hugely Successful First 100 Days," *Business Week*, May 14, 2001, p. 59.

18. James Carney, Massimo Calabresi, Jay Branegan, John

F. Dickerson, Paul Quinn-Judge, and Thomas Sancton, "Mission to Europe," *Time,* June 18, 2001, p. 26.

19. Ibid., pp. 26–27.

20. Peter Katel, Lucy Conger, and Dolly Mascarenas, "Fox's Game Plan," *Time*, September 3, 2001, p. 38.

21. Ibid.

Chapter 7. A Test of Strength and Ability

1. Bob Woodward, *Bush at War* (New York: Simon and Schuster, 2002), p. 41.

2. Ibid., p. 40.

3. Michael Ledeen, *The War Against the Terror Masters* (New York: St. Martin's Press, 2002), p. 35.

4. Ibid., p. 11.

5. Ibid., p. 36.

6. Ibid., p. 44.

7. "Address to a Joint Session of Congress and the American People," The White House Internet site, (September 20, 2001), <http://www.whitehouse.gov/news/releases/2001/09/print/20010920-8.html> (June 10, 2003).

8. Woodward, p. 67.

9. Kevin Flynn, "The Lost Brothers," *A Nation Challenged: A Visual History of 9/11 and Its Aftermath* (New York: Callaway, 2002), p. 82.

10. Woodward, p. 69.

11. Robert D. Mcfadden, "Bush Leads Prayer, Visits Aid Crews," *New York Times*, September 15, 2001, p. A1.

12. Woodward, p. 73.

13. David Masci and Patrick Marshall, "Civil Liberties and the War Against Terrorism: An Overview," in *The Terrorist Attack on America*, Mary E. Williams, ed. (Farmington Hills, Mich.: Greenhaven Press, 2003), pp. 100–101.

14. Ibid., p. 98.

15. Joseph I. Lieberman, "Military Tribunals Need Not Erode Civil Liberties," in *The Terrorist Attack on America*, Mary E. Williams, ed. (Farmington Hills, Mich.: Greenhaven Press, 2003), p. 120.

16. Masci and Marshall, p. 98.

17. Woodward, pp. 313–314.

18. Ibid., p. 316.

Chapter 8. Dealing With Domestic Issues

1. Fe Conway, Karen Yourish, and Josh Ulick, "A Missing Piece . . . in a National Puzzle," *Newsweek*, November 12, 2001, p. 33.

2. Geoffrey Cowley and Anne Underwood, "How Little We Really Know," *Newsweek*, November 12, 2001, p. 36.

3. Don Foster, "The Message in the Anthrax," *Vanity Fair*, October 2003, p. 182.

4. Ibid., p. 200.

5. John Bohannon, "From Bioweapons Backwater to Main Attraction," *Science*, April 18, 2003, p. 414.

6. Foster, p. 200.

7. "U.S. Unemployment Jumps," CNN Internet site, December 7, 2001, <http://www.money.cnn.com/2001/12/07/economy/economy/> (June 25, 2002).

Chapter 9. War on Iraq and on Terrorism

1. "President Delivers State of the Union Address," The White House Internet site, January 2001, <http://www.white house.gov/news/releases/2002/01/20020129-11.html> (June 29, 2001).

2. "Bush's 'Evil Axis' Comment Stirs Critics," BBC News Internet site, February 2, 2002, <http://www.bbc.co.uk/hi/english/world/americas/newsid_1796000/179034.stm> (June 29, 2002).

3. "Disarming Iraq: The Case Against Saddam Hussein," Foreword, *Congressional Digest*, December 2002, p. 289.

4. Michael Elliott, Massimo Calabresi, John F. Dickerson, Mark Thompson, Scott MacLeod, J.F.O. McAllister, and Marguerite Michaels, "Who's With Him?" *Time*, March 3, 2003, p. 30.

5. "Disarming Iraq," p. 289.

6. Ibid.

7. Kevin Whitelaw, Mark Mazzatti, and Thomas Omestad, "Why War?" *U.S. News and World Report*, October 14, 2003, p. 25.

8. Evan Thomas, Melinda Liu, B.J. Lee, George Wehrfritz, Hideko Takayama, Eve Conant, and Michael Hirsh, "Women, Wine, and Weapons," *Newsweek*, January 13, 2003, p. 25.

9. Michael Hirsh, Melinda Liu, George Wehrfritz, Tamara Lipper, and John Barry, "Kim is the Key Danger . . .," *Newsweek*, January 13, 2003, p. 30.

10. "Disarming Iraq," p. 289.

11. "President Delivers 'State of the Union,'" The White House Internet site, January 2003, <http://www/whitehouse. gov/news/releases/2003/01/20030128-19.html> (July 11, 2003).

12. "President Bush Announces Combat Operations in Iraq Have Ended," The White House Internet site, May 2003, <http://www.whitehouse.gov/news/releases/2003/05/iraq/ 200305 01-15.html> (June 10, 2003).

13. Tom Raum, "Rice Says CIA Cleared Bush's State of the Union Speech," New Jersey Internet site, July 11, 2003, <http://www.nj.com/newsflash/international/index.ssf?/ cgi. . ./getsory_ ssf.cgi?a0519_BC_US-Ira> (July 11, 2003).

14. Ibid.

15. Ibid.

16. Scott Lindlaw, "Bush Insists Iraq Had Weapons Program, White House Asks Patience During Search," Boston Internet site, June 9, 2003, <http://www.boston.com/ dailynews/160/wash/Bush_insists_Iraq_had_weapons_P.shtml> (June 10, 2003).

17. S. Frederick Starr, "A Sweet Sixteen," *National Review*, August 11, 2003, pp. 21–22.

18. Daniel Bergner, "Where the Enemy is Everywhere and Nowhere," *New York Times Magazine*, July 20, 2003, pp. 40–41.

19. Starr, p. 22.

20. Ibid.

21. Ibid.

22. Ibid.

23. Ibid., p. 23.

24. Bergner, p. 42.

Chapter 10. The Right Man for the Job

1. Chitra Ragavan and Ann M. Wakefield, "Insecurity Blues," *U.S. News and World Report*, March 10, 2003, p. 33.

2. Adam Cohen, James Carney, Douglas Waller, Adam Zagorin, and Steve Barnes, "Who Swiped the Surplus?" *Time*, September 3, 2001, p. 30.

3. Kenneth T. Walsh, Mark Mazzetti, Kevin Whitlaw, and Jeffrey L. Sheler, "Sticking to His Guns," *U.S. News and World Report*, March 10, 2003, p. 18.

4. Ibid., pp. 18–19.

5. Ibid., p. 16.

FURTHER READING

Bausum, Ann. *Our Country's Presidents*. New York: National Geographic Society, 2001.

Bush, George W. and Mickey Herskowitz. *A Charge to Keep*. New York: William Morrow and Company, 1999.

Gormley, Beatrice. *President George W. Bush: Our 43rd President*. New York: Aladdin Paperbacks, 2001.

McNeese, Tim. *George W. Bush: First President of the New Century*. New York: Morgan Reynolds, Inc., 2001.

INTERNET ADDRESSES

The American Presidency, Grolier Encyclopedia
<http://gi.grolier.com/presidents/preshome.html>

George Bush Presidential Library and Museum
<http://bushlibrary.tamu.edu>

The White House
<http://www.whitehouse.gov>

Places to Visit

Texas

George Bush Presidential Library and Museum. College Station. 979-691-4000. The museum contains personal papers, photographs, videos, and other researchable materials about forty-first President George Bush. It also features material about First Lady Barbara Bush and the Bush family. Open every day, except Thanksgiving Day, Christmas Day, New Year's Day.

Texas Governor's Mansion. Austin. 512-463-5516. Built in 1856, the mansion is the most historic house in Texas. It is also the oldest continuously occupied executive residence west of the Mississippi. Tours every twenty minutes. Open Monday through Thursday.

The Ballpark in Arlington. Arlington. 817-273-5222. Home stadium of the Texas Rangers, this state-of-the-art, baseball-only facility opened in 1994. The site includes a baseball museum, children's learning center, youth baseball park, and twelve-acre lake.

Massachusetts

Phillips Academy. Andover. The academy is a coeducational independent high school about twenty-five miles north of Boston. Founded in 1778, it is the nation's oldest incorporated boarding school. The complex also features the Robert S. Peabody Museum of Archaeology and the Addison Gallery of American Art.

INDEX